# Endangered
# Animals

**Kestrel,** Mauritius **– Mulgara**

GROLIER
EDUCATIONAL

**Published 2002 by Grolier Educational, Danbury, CT 06816**

This edition published exclusively for the school and library market

Produced by Andromeda Oxford Limited
11–13 The Vineyard, Abingdon,
Oxon OX14 3PX, U.K.
www.andromeda.co.uk

**Principal Contributors:** *Amy-Jane Beer, Andrew Campbell, Robert and Valerie Davies, John Dawes, Jonathan Elphick, Tim Halliday, Pat Morris. Further contributions by David Capper and John Woodward*

**Project Director:** *Graham Bateman*
**Managing Editors:** *Shaun Barrington, Jo Newson*
**Editor:** *Penelope Mathias*
**Art Editor and Designer:** *Steve McCurdy*
**Cartographic Editor:** *Tim Williams*
**Editorial Assistant:** *Marian Dreier*
**Picture Manager:** *Claire Turner*
**Production:** *Clive Sparling*
**Indexers:** *Indexing Specialists, Hove, East Sussex*

Reproduction by A. T. Color, Milan
Printing by H & Y Printing Ltd., Hong Kong

Set ISBN 0-7172-5584-0

**Library of Congress Cataloging-in-Publication Data**

Endangered animals.
     p. cm.
    Contents: v. 1. What is an endangered animal? -- v. 2. Addax - blackbuck -- v. 3. Boa, Jamaican - danio, barred -- v. 4. Darter, Watercress - frog, gastric brooding -- v. 5. Frog, green and golden bell - kestrel, lesser -- v. 6. Kestrel, Mauritius - Mulgara -- v. 7. Murrelet, Japanese - Pupfish, Devil's Hole -- v. 8. Pygmy-possum, mountain - Siskin, red -- v. 9. Skink, pygmy blue-tongued - tragopan, Temminck's -- v. 10. Tree-kangaroo, Goodfellow's - zebra, mountain.
   ISBN 0-7172-5584-0 (set : alk. paper) -- ISBN 0-7172-5585-9 (v. 1 : alk. paper) – ISBN 0-7172-5586-7 (v. 2 : alk. paper) -- ISBN 0-7172-5587-5 (v. 3 : alk. paper) – ISBN 0-7172-5588-3 (v. 4 : alk. paper) -- ISBN 0-7172-5589-1 (v. 5 : alk. paper) – ISBN 0-7172-5590-5 (v. 6 : alk. paper) -- ISBN 0-7172-5591-3 (v. 7 : alk. paper) – ISBN 0-7172-5592-1 (v. 8 : alk. paper) -- ISBN 0-7172-5593-X (v. 9 : alk. paper) – ISBN 0-7172-5594-8 (v. 10 : alk. paper)
   1. Endangered species--Juvenile literature. [1. Endangered species.] I. Grolier Educational (Firm)

QL83 .E54 2001
333.95'42--dc21

00-069134

# Contents

# About This Set

Endangered Animals is a 10-volume set that highlights and explains the threats to animal species across the world. Habitat loss is one major threat; another is the introduction of species into areas where they do not normally live.

Examples of different animals facing a range of problems have been chosen to include all the major animal groups. Fish, reptiles, amphibians, and insects and invertebrates are included as well as mammals and birds. Some species may have very large populations, but they nevertheless face problems. Some are already extinct.

Volume 1—What Is an Endangered Animal?—explains how scientists classify animals, the reasons why they are endangered, and what conservationists are doing about it. Cross-references in the text (volume number followed by page number) show relevant pages in the set.

Volumes 2 to 10 contain individual species entries arranged in alphabetical order. Each entry is a double-page spread with a data panel summarizing key facts and a locator map showing its range.

Look for a particular species by its common name, listed in alphabetical order on the Contents page of each book. (Page references for both common and scientific names are in the full set index at the back of each book.) When you have found the species that interests you, you can find related entries by looking first in the data panel. If an animal listed under Related endangered species has an asterisk (*) next to its name, it has its own separate entry. You can also check the cross-references at the bottom of the left-hand page, which refer to entries in other volumes. (For example, "Finch, Gouldian **4:** 74" means that the two-page entry about the Gouldian finch starts on page 74 of Volume 4.) The cross-reference is usually made to an animal that is in the same genus or family as the species you are reading about; but a species may appear here because it is from the same part of the world or faces the same threats.

Each book ends with a glossary of terms, lists of useful publications and websites, and a full set index.

# **Kestrel,** Mauritius

### *Falco punctatus*

*Reduced to a population of just four wild birds by 1974, the Mauritius kestrel has clawed its way back from the edge of extinction to become a spectacular success story.*

The island of Mauritius in the Indian Ocean will always be notorious as the former home of the dodo: the universal symbol of extinction. Until recently the Mauritius kestrel seemed bound to suffer the same fate since its numbers had reached a point from which recovery seemed impossible.

The Mauritius kestrel hunts like a short-winged sparrowhawk. Its relatively short wings give it the maneuverability to pursue prey beneath the canopy of dense evergreen forest that once covered much of the island. It usually hunts from a perch, moving swiftly and swerving through the branches to snatch prey (songbirds, dragonflies, or lizards) from the air or the trees. Among its favorite targets are the iridescent green geckos found only on Mauritius; the kestrel is expert at locating them as they bask, immobile in the sun. Occasionally, it hovers to pinpoint prey in low vegetation, but its wings are not really adapted to the task. It is a bird of the forests. As the forests were felled to provide farmland for a growing population, the kestrel gradually disappeared.

### **Relentless Decline**

Mauritius kestrels have never been abundant. Each breeding pair occupies a large territory, and the entire island is no bigger than a large city. At most there were probably only 1,000 birds. By the 1970s rampant deforestation had eliminated most native forest cover, leaving only a few pockets of habitat in rocky gorges on the southwest of the island. The kestrels were also shot by farmers—who believed they stole poultry— and poisoned by pesticides. Their tree nesting sites

were vulnerable to the egg-thieving nonnative macaque monkeys, as well as introduced cats, rats, and mongoose. It was a deadly combination, and by 1974 there were just four birds.

That season one pair nested in a tree in the usual way, but their nest was raided by monkeys. For some reason the other pair chose to nest in a hole in a sheer cliff. The choice of this unusual nesting site saved the species because the cliff face was monkey-proof. Three chicks fledged, and for the first time in years the Mauritius kestrel population increased. The young birds adopted the

4

**See also:** Introductions **1:** 54; Captive Breeding **1:** 87; Reintroduction **1:** 92; Kestrel, Lesser **5:** 94

**Mauritius kestrels** *are currently being studied to determine their genetic variation so that their genetic diversity can be maintained.*

## DATA PANEL

**Mauritius kestrel**

*Falco punctatus*

**Family:** Falconidae

**World population:** About 500–800 birds

**Distribution:** Island of Mauritius in the southwestern Indian Ocean

**Habitat:** Primarily evergreen subtropical forest, but captive-bred birds released into the wild have colonized degraded secondary forest and scrub

**Size:** Length: 8–10 in (20–26 cm). Weight: male 6 oz (178 g); female 8 oz (231 g)

**Form:** Small and stocky, with long legs and tail; unusually short, rounded wings for a kestrel. Female bigger than male. Black-barred, chestnut-colored upperparts, black-flecked white underparts, black eye with typical dark falcon "moustache" below; yellow skin on legs and at base of bill. Juvenile has blue-gray facial skin

**Diet:** Lizards (mainly tree-climbing geckos), small birds, large insects, and introduced mice and shrews

**Breeding:** Naturally nests in tree cavities, but may now use cliff sites and nest boxes; lays 2–5 (usually 3) eggs in August–November; young hatch after 4 weeks

**Related endangered species:** Seychelles kestrel *(Falco araea)* VU; lesser kestrel *(F. naumanni)** VU;

**Status:** IUCN VU; CITES I and II

cliff-nesting habit when they matured, and by 1976 they had boosted the population to 15 birds.

## Revival

Early attempts to breed Mauritius kestrels in captivity ended in failure. The first success came in 1984, and since then many birds have been bred in captivity both in Mauritius and at the World Center for Birds of Prey in Boise, Idaho. By 1993 there were 200 birds.

The object was always to reintroduce the birds to the wild. Released captive-bred birds initially had trouble establishing territories in areas where there were wild kestrels; only about 50 percent of birds released in prime habitat survived their first year.

It was assumed that Mauritius kestrels would not thrive in other types of terrain, but the captive-bred birds have proved adaptable.

Released into areas of degraded secondary forest, their survival rate after a year is about 80 percent. By the end of the 1999 to 2000 breeding season there were three subpopulations, including between 145 and 200 breeding pairs. At first the birds were sustained by supplementary feeding, nest-guarding, predator control, and other conservation measures. But since 1994 there have been no more reintroductions, and apart from careful monitoring, the kestrels have virtually been left to their own devices.

The Mauritius kestrel will never be quite safe: Its total population is so small that it will always be vulnerable to natural disasters such as tropical storms and infectious diseases. However, its story shows what can be done, given the will and a little luck.

**5**

# Kite, Red

*Milvus milvus*

*After an apparently relentless decline stretching over three or four centuries, the red kite is staging a comeback in the northwest of its range, thanks largely to the efforts of conservationists.*

Big, beautiful, and almost balletic in its mastery of the sky, the red kite is one of the world's most spectacular raptors. Instantly identifiable by its rich, chestnut plumage and forked tail, it flies with a buoyant, airy grace that seems to defy gravity. It flourishes particularly in open, half-wild country with scattered woodlands, where it can locate food from the air and find plenty of trees for roosting.

At one time the kite was a common sight over much of Europe, even in major cities, for although it is a hunter, its real talent lies in scavenging easy meals from carcasses and refuse dumps. Back in the 16th century there were rich pickings to be had from every back alley, and the practice of allowing farm animals to roam over unfenced land ensured a steady supply of carrion. Yet by the end of the Middle Ages it was on the brink of a long, slow decline in numbers.

It disappeared from the cities first. Improved hygiene eliminated edible garbage from the streets. Like many other raptors, the kite was declared vermin, but its leisurely flight style made it an easier target than most. As guns became widespread during the 18th and 19th centuries, the red kite was gradually shot out of the skies. Others were trapped or poisoned; since they feed from carcasses, they can fall victim to poisoned bait laid out for other animals.

At the same time, agriculture was becoming more scientific, and farmers were abandoning the old ways in favor of more intensive systems. In the lowlands the supply of carrion began to dry up; and when chemical pesticides came into common use, live prey began to disappear too. Gradually, the kites retreated to the mountains and moors, where they could still find food and secure nesting sites.

In many places they are still declining. In eastern Europe the intensification of agriculture following land privatization has reduced their habitat. Yet the most endangered population is the distinctive, smaller race that once flourished on the Cape Verde Islands, off West Africa. Its numbers began to dwindle in the 1960s, partly because of the virtual destruction of the natural ecosystem on many of the islands and partly because the red kites were interbreeding with similar black kites. By the year 2000 the population had crashed to just four birds. Barring a virtual miracle, the Cape Verde red kite will be extinct within five years.

## Welsh Revival

In sharp contrast, conservation efforts in northwestern Europe have led to a kite revival. In Britain, for example, a tiny relict population of red kites managed to survive in the mountains of central Wales, where they were able to exploit a steady supply of rabbit and sheep carcasses. Yet in 1903, when conservation

**See also:** Communities and Ecosystems **1:** 22; Sea-Eagle, Steller's **8:** 64

began, they were on the edge of extinction, with only 12 birds left. Since then intensive research, better protection, supplementary feeding, and the cooperation of local farmers have gradually enabled the Welsh kites to bounce back. By 2000 there were some 800 individuals, with 259 breeding pairs. Meanwhile, kites from southern Sweden and northern Spain have been introduced into hill country in England and Scotland, with similar success.

The Welsh experience shows that the red kite is a survivor; given the right conditions, it can breed its way back from near-oblivion. Other countries in northwestern Europe are reporting similar increases, which partly offset the losses in other parts of its range. Yet ultimately its future may depend on the survival of another endangered species: the organic farmer, whose pesticide-free fields nurture the wild plants and insects that form the basis of the ecosystem on which the bird depends.

**The red kite** *includes carrion in its diet and is susceptible to both deliberate and accidental poisoning of carcasses.*

## DATA PANEL

**Red kite**

*Milvus milvus*

**Family:** Accipitridae

**World population:** 19,000–32,000 breeding pairs

**Distribution:** From western Russia west to Wales, Spain, and the Cape Verde Islands; from southern Sweden south to Sicily and northwestern Morocco

**Habitat:** Mixed country, often hilly, with woodland for nesting and meadows, lakes, and rivers

**Size:** Length: 24–26 in (60–66 cm); wingspan: 5.7–6.4 ft (1.8–2 m). Weight: 1.8–2.9 lb (0.8–1.3 kg); females larger than males

**Form:** Sleek, graceful bird of prey with long wings, long, deeply forked tail, and feathered legs. Gray-white head; red-brown upperparts with black wingtips; rich chestnut underparts and tail; large, pale patches on undersides of outer wings. Bright yellow eyes, black-tipped yellow bill, yellow feet, black talons

**Diet:** Birds, small mammals, fish, large insects, earthworms, carrion, and scraps

**Breeding:** In March–May 2–4 eggs are laid in a nest of sticks and mud, often incorporating scraps of paper, plastic, or cloth, high in a tall tree or, rarely, on a cliff. The nest is often built on top of an abandoned buzzard's or crow's nest, and the same site is often reused every year for decades. The female incubates the eggs for 31–32 days, and the chicks fledge after 48–60 days

**Related endangered species:** Many birds of prey in the family Accipitridae, including the Cuban kite (*Chondrohierax wilsonii*) CR and the white-collared kite (*Leptodon forbesi*) CR

**Status:** Not listed by IUCN; CITES II

Cape Verde

# Kiwi, Brown

### *Apteryx mantelli*

*The mainland populations of the unique brown kiwi–found only in New Zealand–have suffered huge declines in the 20th century, mainly due to plundering by introduced predators.*

**The female brown kiwi** *lays large eggs: Each egg weighs as much as 20 percent of her body weight.*

With its shaggy, hairlike plumage, a plump, round body, a lack of visible tail or wings, and an ability to track down food in the dead of night, kiwis resemble nocturnal mammals rather than typical birds. Like many mammals, they also rest and shelter their young in burrows and mark their boundaries with strong-smelling droppings; the bristly modified feathers at the base of the bill serve as whiskers for feeling in the dark. Isolated for millions of years on New Zealand—where there are no native mammals except bats—the brown kiwi has occupied a niche that elsewhere would be filled by a mammal.

Kiwis are the smallest living ratites—a group of flightless birds that includes the ostrich, rheas, cassowaries, and the emu, none of which are nocturnal. Until recently ornithologists recognized three species of kiwi: the little spotted kiwi, the brown kiwi, and the great spotted kiwi. Genetic research has led to the brown kiwi being split into two distinct species, the brown kiwi and the tokoeka of a few areas in South Island. The Maori name kiwi comes from the shrill call of males, which punctuates the night, especially during the breeding season.

### Long-Term Decline

Brown kiwis were once widespread throughout North Island and the northern part of South Island. Although they were hunted by the Maori—who had colonized New Zealand from the Pacific by the 12th century—this probably had little effect on overall numbers. It was not until the European settlers arrived in the mid-19th century that persecution of the birds began in earnest, as hunters tried to satisfy the demand for kiwi plumage by the clothing trade. A law banning the hunting, capture, or killing of kiwis was passed in 1908, but the pace of land clearance for agriculture and settlements destroyed much of the kiwi's forest habitat. The birds' fate was further sealed by the introduction of predatory mammals such as cats, dogs, and stoats. As a result of the combined threats, large-scale losses of brown kiwis occurred.

Researchers think that numbers of brown kiwis have fallen by at least 90 percent over the last 100 years and continue to decline at about 6 percent every year (in studied sites). This represents the halving of the population each decade. However, the species' overall decline is probably below 80 percent, thanks to the stability of the populations introduced to islands where predators are removed—and also to effective predator control in mainland sites.

The main threat facing the brown kiwi is still introduced predators, especially since it evolved with no native predators. At least 94 percent of kiwi chicks die before they reach breeding age (about 14 months for males and two years for females). Half of this mortality is due to predation. The other main cause of decline is the clearance of native forest, which threatens small, isolated populations. Many kiwis also

8

**See also:** The Feather Trade **1:** 46; Introductions **1:** 54; Cassowary, Southern **3:** 28

**The brown kiwi** *is nocturnal and has tiny, poorly developed eyes that enable it to see only a few yards ahead. Unusually for a bird, it detects its prey by smell.*

used to die in traps set to catch predators or possums; animals reached plague proportions in some areas. Today this is avoided by raising traps above the ground so that the kiwis do not stumble upon them.

## Conservation

Conservationists have an accurate picture of kiwi populations thanks to an intensive, nationally coordinated program of monitoring. By culling introduced predators and by removing eggs and hand-rearing the young to an age when they can fend off attacks, key populations have been helped. Continued protection is needed to save the brown kiwi.

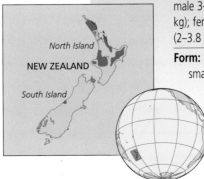

North Island

NEW ZEALAND

South Island

### DATA PANEL

**Brown kiwi**

*Apteryx mantelli*

**Family:** Apterygidae

**World population:** About 35,000 birds

**Distribution:** North Island in Northland; Coromandel Peninsula from Gisborne to northern Ruahine Range, and Tongariro to Taranaki. Introduced to Little Barrier, Kawau, and Pounui Islands. Isolated population on Okarito, South Island, may be a separate species with Critical status

**Habitat:** Subtropical and temperate forests; regenerating forest, shrubland, pine plantations, and pastureland

**Size:** Length: 16 in (40 cm). Weight: male 3–6.5 lb (1.4–3 kg); female 4.5–8 lb (2–3.8 kg)

**Form:** Bird the size of a small dog; small head; long, slightly downcurved bill with bristles at base; long neck (usually drawn in); rotund body covered with coarse, hairlike plumage that is dark gray-brown with red-brown streaks; rudimentary wing stubs in plumage; strong legs; 4 toes on each foot

**Diet:** Invertebrates in soil and leaf litter, especially earthworms, spiders, and insects; also fruit, seeds, and leaves

**Breeding:** Female lays 1 or 2 very large eggs in August–September in burrow or natural cavity; egg(s) incubated by male for 11–12 weeks; chick(s) independent at 14–20 days; fully grown by 20 months

**Related endangered species:** Great spotted kiwi (*Apteryx haastii*) VU; little spotted kiwi (*A. owenii*) VU; tokoeka (*A. australis*) VU

**Status:** IUCN EN; not listed by CITES

# Koala

*Phascolarctos cinereus*

*The koala has enjoyed considerable conservation success. However, although it is no longer threatened with extinction, managing the remaining populations is proving problematic for conservationists.*

Koalas manage to survive on a diet that no other mammal will touch—eucalyptus leaves. Tough, dry, and with a very low nutritional value, the leaves also contain indigestible materials and compounds that are highly poisonous to most other animals. Koalas are able to exist on this poor diet by having efficient digestive systems that will not only break down the toxins but also extract every available calorie. They also conserve energy by spending up to 20 hours a day resting. Until the arrival of European settlers in Australia in the late 18th century the ability of the koala to eke out a living from a food that no other animal could eat meant that it was a highly successful animal, well adapted to its diet and environment.

## Consequences of Colonization

European settlement brought a number of threats to Australia's native wildlife. It destroyed the natural habitat and caused a marked increase in forest fires. The koala was also hunted for its fur. By the early 20th century koalas were facing a very real threat of extinction. Disaster was narrowly averted when the koala was made a nationally protected species in 1927. The koala has now returned to much of its original range; but because its habitat is patchy, it will never be as common as it once was. Although the koala as a species is out of immediate danger, individuals and localized populations are still threatened. Many koalas are killed on the roads or attacked by dogs, and forest fires can wipe out whole colonies at a time.

## Victims of Success

The biggest problem is the patchy, isolated nature of the remaining koala habitat. The species responds so well to conservation that protected populations often increase to the point where the animals begin to damage the trees that they rely on for survival. Yet surplus animals cannot easily disperse if their forest home is surrounded by urban development or vast areas of open pastureland, as is now the case in much of eastern Australia. In overcrowded

---

## DATA PANEL

**Koala**

*Phascolarctos cinereus*

**Family:** Phascolarctidae

**World population:** About 40,000, but estimates vary widely and are controversial

**Distribution:** Eastern Australia

**Habitat:** Eucalyptus forests below 2,000 ft (600 m)

**Size:** Length head/body: 28–31 in (72–78 cm); animals from south of range larger than those in north. Weight: 11–24 lb (5–11 kg); males can be half as heavy again as females

**Form:** Stout, bearlike animal with thick, woolly, grayish-brown fur on back, fading to white on belly. Head large with rounded furry ears, beady black eyes, and large black nose. Legs short with 5 large claws on each foot.

Tail short and stumpy. Female has pouch that opens to the rear

**Diet:** Leaves of various species of eucalyptus

**Breeding:** Single young (occasionally twins) born in midsummer after gestation of 25–30 days; young spend 5–7 months in pouch, weaned at 6–12 months; mature at 2 years. Life span up to 20 years

**Related endangered species:** No close relatives, but the northern hairy-nosed wombat *(Lasiorhinus krefftii)** of northeastern Australia is listed as CR

**Status:** IUCN LRnt; not listed by CITES

AUSTRALIA

**See also:** Specialization 1: 28; Wombat, Northern Hairy-Nosed 10: 76

conditions the koala is especially vulnerable to a disease caused by the *Chlamydia psittaci* bacterium. Conservation programs therefore face the difficult task of establishing healthy koala populations without creating overpopulated, disease-ridden colonies in which surplus animals have to be culled.

The least damaging solution is to move the excess koalas to other areas of suitable habitat. However, after 200 years of logging, development, and clearance for agriculture there are very few large areas of eucalyptus forest available. Consequently, koalas are often moved to other isolated patches of woodland where they soon become overcrowded again. The only real solution is to create "corridors" of habitat linking the isolated patches so that koala populations can

**Koalas,** *like other Australian marsupials, are born very early and suckled by their mother—often in a pouch—for the first months of life. Koala young are weaned on to "pap," a special form of the mother's droppings that provides the baby with the gut bacteria it needs to digest eucalyptus leaves.*

spread themselves more evenly. Tracts of suitable land connecting isolated koala populations would benefit the species in other ways: When koala colonies are decimated by natural events such as forest fires or outbreaks of *Chlamydia*, koalas dispersing from other areas would be able to recolonize the affected sites.

**11**

# Komodo Dragon

## *Varanus komodoensis*

*Known locally as* buaja daret *("land crocodiles"), these giant lizards were named after the mythical dragon because of their size and fierce predatory nature.*

It seems inconceivable that the enormous Komodo dragon could remain unknown (at least to western scientists) until the early 20th century. Referred to locally as the *ora* or *buaja daret* ("land crocodile"), early reported sightings were probably dismissed as superstition or simply as crocodiles. In 1912 a Dutch pilot, having swum ashore to the island of Komodo after crashing in the sea, reported seeing them; further investigation verified their existence. The first scientific description was by Major P. A. Ouwens, director of the botanical gardens in Buitenzorg, Java, in 1912. Soon afterward a government order closed the area in which they were found and limited the number of specimens allowed to go to zoos.

The Komodo dragon is found only on Komodo and the neighboring islands of Rinca, Padar, and western Flores. Some of the populations are probably transient—they are powerful swimmers and go from island to island in search of food. The total area of their natural habitat is roughly 390 square miles (1,000 sq. km), and it is generally hot, with an average daytime temperature of 80°F (27°C) or higher. Usually conditions are very dry, too, apart from a short monsoon season, when the Komodo dragons use pools caused by rain for wallowing. During hot weather and overnight they take to burrows.

Komodo dragons are top predators in their range. Adults will tackle anything, including deer, pigs, and goats. Occasionally even humans are said to feature in the diet. They are armed with a strong tail as well as powerful limbs and claws. Their teeth are serrated like those of sharks and can easily rip a carcass. They also produce bacteria that cause blood poisoning and death. Prey that is not killed immediately often dies later. Komodo dragons can scent the carrion up to

Borneo
Sulawesi
INDONESIA
Java
Sumbawa
Flores
Sumba
Timor

## DATA PANEL

**Komodo dragon**

***Varanus komodoensis***

**Family:** Varanidae

**World population:** 3,000–5,000 in the wild

**Distribution:** Indonesia; islands of Komodo, Rinca, Padar, and western Flores

**Habitat:** Lowland islands, arid forest, and savanna

**Size:** Length: males over 8 ft (2.4 m); females 7 ft (2.1 m). Weight: males 200 lb (90 kg); females 150 lb (67 kg)

**Form:** Lizard with large, bulky body and powerful tail, strong limbs, and claws. Rough scales give a beaded appearance. External ear openings are visible on each side of the head. Sharp teeth for ripping carcasses. Coloration is brown, black, reddish brown, or gray

**Diet:** Hatchlings and juveniles eat insects, reptiles, eggs, small rodents, and birds. Adults eat deer, pigs, goats, possibly water buffalo, and reputedly, humans

**Breeding:** Up to 30 eggs, buried. Incubation period about 8 months

**Related endangered species:** Gray's monitor lizard (*Varanus olivaceus*) VU

**Status:** IUCN VU; CITES I

**See also:** The History of Reptiles **1:** 73; Gila Monster **5:** 28; Whiptail, St. Lucia **10:** 60

5 miles (8 km) away and come to gather at the site of the death.

The Indonesian government regards Komodo dragons as a national asset, and they are protected. Hunting is strictly forbidden; trade in Komodos (or their parts) is banned under CITES. Tourists on Komodo are carefully controlled to prevent disturbance. The islands of Padar and Rinca are nature reserves where no tourists are allowed. However, Komodo dragons have been smuggled. In 1998 a Malaysian was arrested in Mexico City after investigation by the United States Fish and Wildlife Service, and Komodo dragons were seized.

## Protecting the Species

The main threat to Komodo dragons comes from habitat destruction and the poaching of their prey by inhabitants on Komodo Island. Padar and Rinca are uninhabited, so this is not a problem; however, there, as on Komodo, natural fires destroy the plants and animals on which the dragons depend. Recent reports claim that many specimens on Komodo are emaciated from lack of food.

The first captive-breeding attempt was carried out in the National Zoo, Washington, in 1992, when 13 out of a clutch of 26 eggs hatched; this was followed by two successful hatchings at Cincinnati Zoo in 1993. Currently around 300 specimens are held in zoos worldwide; 186 of the specimens are juveniles bred in captivity. This is encouraging, but many zoos are unable to set up breeding groups due to lack of space. Zoo populations are seen as a "reservoir" from which specimens could be reintroduced into the wild. No further introductions will be made, however, until the genetic makeup of wild and captive-bred specimens has been studied, since variations between the two have been observed.

**The Komodo dragon** *is a giant lizard about 8 feet (2.4 m) long. The largest recorded example, which was displayed in Saint Louis in the 1930s, measured 10.2 feet (3 m) and weighed over 350 pounds (160 kg).*

# Kouprey

### Bos sauveli

*The kouprey is one of the world's rarest mammals, inhabiting areas affected by war and forest clearance. This shy, forest-dwelling ox is now almost certainly on the very brink of extinction.*

The kouprey has probably always been rather scarce; indeed, it remained unknown to science until 1937, when horns mounted in the home of a French veterinarian were recognized as something rather special by a visiting naturalist. The horns turned out to come from a massive, gray forest ox. A live specimen was subsequently captured and taken to Vincennes Zoo near Paris, where it was officially described. So far, this is the only kouprey that has ever been successfully captured alive.

In the years following the species' discovery a few limited studies of wild koupreys were carried out, and it seems that even at this time there were probably no more than 1,000 animals, living in Cambodia (also known as Kampuchea), Vietnam, Laos, Thailand, and Malaysia. By the mid-1970s, after prolonged military action in the region, numbers had plummeted so far that for a time it was thought the kouprey might already be extinct. Fortunately this was not the case. Today most reports of kouprey sightings come from soldiers or villagers and are difficult to verify; some could be cases of mistaken identity. Even so, scientists are confident that the kouprey is distinctive enough for at least some sightings to be genuine.

Male koupreys are easy to identify, since they have a large flap of skin, called a dewlap, dangling from the throat. In some males the dewlap almost touches the ground. Both males and females have horns, which in females look distinctively lyre-shaped when seen from the front. Those of the males, which can grow up to 32 inches (80 cm) long, curve forward then upward and have strangely contorted ends. The tips cannot be rubbed smooth as in most other horned animals, so they end up looking oddly frayed.

These days most of the population is thought to live in Cambodia, and in the early 1960s the kouprey was designated the country's national animal. Little is known about the koupreys' day-to-day life, but what information there is suggests that they live in small, casual herds, with animals coming and going, and often mixing with other wild or feral cattle such as banteng and water buffalo. Koupreys wander widely in search of suitable food, mostly grasses, and spend a lot of time around watering holes and salt licks. There are reports that they move to higher altitudes during the rainy season, but whether or not this is a regular migration is not known. The rainy season also sees a change in the composition of the herds, with males leaving to wander

## DATA PANEL

**Kouprey (Cambodian forest ox)**

***Bos sauveli***

**Family:** Bovidae

**World population:** Fewer than 300

**Distribution:** Cambodia and Vietnam. Formerly Malaysia and Thailand

**Habitat:** Forest edges and thickets in rolling hill country, retreating to denser forests

**Size:** Length: 7–7.2 ft (2.1–2.2 m); height at shoulder: 5.5–6.2 ft (1.7–1.9 m). Weight: up to 1,500–2,000 lb (700–910 kg)

**Form:** A large, gray ox with distinctive horns, lyre-shaped in females, curved with frayed edges in males

**Diet:** Mostly grasses, some leaves

**Breeding:** Single calf born between December and February. May live for about 20 years

**Related endangered species:** Lowland anoa *(Bubalus depressicornis)* EN; mountain anoa *(B. quarlesi)*\* EN; wild yak *(Bos grunniens)*\* VU; banteng *(B. javanicus)*\* EN

**Status:** IUCN CR; CITES I

**See also:** War **1:** 47; Disease **1:** 55; Anoa, Mountain **2:** 20; Banteng **2:** 50; Gaur **5:** 18

alone or as part of a bachelor group. The females remain together in small groups except when they are due to give birth, when they wander off alone, only returning to the group when the calf is about four weeks old.

## Efforts to Save the Species

The fact that koupreys mingle so readily with other cattle, including feral and domestic stock, at one time led to speculation that they may have originated as a hybrid between domestic stock and a species of wild cattle such as the guar or banteng. However, the kouprey has so many distinguishing features that few scientists these days would question its status as a genuine natural species. Contact with domestic cows should in fact be discouraged, since the spread of cattle diseases into the wild kouprey population could be disastrous. However, there is reason to suppose that koupreys may be resistant to at least one serious

**A big-horned forest ox,** *the kouprey has been unlucky in its distribution. Warfare in Cambodia, its main home, has hampered efforts to preserve it.*

disease of domestic cattle, namely, rinderpest. This possibility has only added impetus to the already determined efforts to save the species, because its immunity might provide a basis for creating a vaccine for domestic cattle.

Despite impressive international cooperation, the sheer scarcity of these shy forest oxen is hindering efforts to monitor and protect them. Logging and forest clearance for agriculture are steadily eroding the edges of the kouprey's forest habitat, and a few animals are still undoubtedly being killed for meat. The only hope would appear to be properly protected reserves and the building up of populations in a captive-breeding program. Without such efforts the future for the kouprey hangs in the balance.

EX
EW
CR
EN
VU
LR
O

**MAMMAL**

# Kudu, Greater

*Tragelaphus strepsiceros*

*The greater kudu is secure in the national parks and protected areas of some African countries but has declined to extinction in other locations.*

The greater kudu is one of the largest antelopes in Africa. It has a distinctive striped coat and a crest of hair along the shoulder. Males have a shaggy mane and spiral horns. The kudu is an animal of open dry forests rather than the dense jungles of central Africa, and it can live without water for long periods. Consequently, large areas of savanna are available to it, including most of Africa south of the Sahara. Although it has never been an abundant animal, in the past the kudu was fairly numerous over this huge area. However, hunting for its meat and its horns has meant that it is now rare or extinct in many places, particularly in the northern part of its range.

Kudus are browsing animals, feeding mainly on leaves. They are active mostly at night, and spend the day standing quietly in the cool of the shade. They disperse widely during the wet season, when there is plenty of food available. In drier periods they tend to congregate in small groups. Unlike some other African antelopes, they do not form large herds, and it is rare to see more than five together at a time.

## Danger from Hunting

Kudus are very athletic, despite their size, and can leap over 6 feet (2 m) into the air. Their large ears are constantly alert for danger, and the animals are difficult to approach closely. Their wariness and athleticism make them a challenge for big-game hunters, who prize their fine spiral horns as trophies. However, kudus often run for only a short distance before stopping to check on the danger that threatens them, a fatal strategy when the threat comes from a hunter with a gun. Many have been shot in this way, especially the larger males. Selective removal of the

---

### DATA PANEL

**Greater kudu**

*Tragelaphus strepsiceros*

**Family:** Bovidae

**World population:** Several thousand

**Distribution:** From Ethiopia and southern Chad to South Africa

**Habitat:** Savanna

**Size:** Length: 6–8 ft (1.8–2.5 m); males slightly larger than females; height at shoulder: 36–54 in (100–150 cm). Weight: male 400–700 lb (190–315 kg); female 260–470 lb (120–215 kg)

**Form:** Tall grayish antelope with up to 12 vertical white stripes on body. Spiral horns (in males only) up to 4.9 ft (1.5 m) long. Females are browner in color and lack horns. Both sexes have crest of hair along the back and down the throat; ears particularly large

**Diet:** Wide range of plants, including grasses, leaves, flowers, and fruit. Diet changes seasonally as a result of the rains. In dry season can make do with whatever is available

**Breeding:** One young born each year, usually in the early part of the wet season, after 9-month gestation; young independent at 6 months; mature at 3 years. Life span over 20 years in captivity

**Related endangered species:** Mountain nyala *(Tragelaphus buxtoni)** EN

**Status:** IUCN LRcd; not listed by CITES

---

**See also:** Hunting **1:** 42; Nyala, Mountain **7:** 18; Gazelle, Dama **5:** 20

finest specimens from the population not only reduces total numbers but also removes the best-adapted individuals. If predation of the healthiest males continues for generations, there is a danger that the males left alone by the hunters may not be the best quality animals genetically and that the species will be weakened as a result.

## Decreasing Numbers

Even the best habitats rarely support more than two or three kudus per square mile. Excessive hunting for their tasty lean meat (as well as for their horns) has reduced their number. In several areas there have been wars and local fighting, and large kudus offer a plentiful supply of meat for hungry soldiers. Moreover,

**A small group of female kudus and young** *stands alert, scanning the savanna for predators. For their size these large antelope are surprisingly agile.*

across the kudu's range much dry bush has now been turned into cultivated land and large areas that would otherwise have supported kudus have been taken over. As a result of shrinking habitat, the remaining animals sometimes take to raiding new farms, leading to them being shot or snared as pests.

Although the species is not at risk of extinction at the moment, the various threats it faces have left the greater kudu endangered in Uganda, Somalia, Chad, and northern Kenya, while in other areas its numbers are also declining.

17

# Lark, Raso

## *Alauda razae*

*With one of the smallest ranges of any bird in the world, the Raso lark—a close relative of the skylark—is critically threatened by adverse changes on the tiny Atlantic island to which it is restricted. Its total population is currently in the low hundreds or fewer.*

The Raso lark is found only on the islet of Raso (or Razo) in the Cape Verde group, 310 miles (500 km) off the west coast of Africa. Volcanic in origin, Raso is low-lying and lacks natural water supplies. It experiences only slight and erratic rainfall that does nothing to relieve the dry conditions. Although the larger islands in the group have human populations, Raso is uninhabited.

Raso is also small—less than 3 square miles (7 sq. km) in area—and suitable breeding habitat for the lark occupies less than half of the islet's total area. Most of the birds feed and breed on a flat expanse of decomposing volcanic lava and soft rocks deposited from hot, lime-rich springs that support a sparse growth of herbaceous plants and low scrub. Although individuals have sometimes been recorded elsewhere

on the island, the Raso lark has never been recorded anywhere beyond its shores.

Raso larks feed on insects and seeds. Analysis of the stomach contents of two birds collected in the late 1960s showed them to contain ants, beetles, seeds, and other vegetable matter, as well as grit, probably swallowed to aid digestion. Since then the larks have been observed using their bills—which are heavier and longer than those of skylarks—to pry pebbles out of the soil, presumably to expose items of food.

An interesting feature of the species is the difference—of almost 21 percent—in the length of the bill in males and females. The gap has probably evolved in response to the island's relatively meager food resources—plants and animals that depend for their existence primarily

## DATA PANEL

**Raso lark (Razo lark)**

*Alauda razae*

**Family:** Alaudidae

**World population:** Fluctuates between 40 and 250 birds

**Distribution:** Found only on the tiny island of Raso, in the Cape Verde Island group in the Atlantic off the west coast of Africa

**Habitat:** Mostly volcanic plains with patches of sparse vegetation, where it feeds and breeds; sometimes ventures farther afield to feed

**Size:** Length: 5 in (13 cm); wingspan: 8.5–10 in (22–26 cm)

**Form:** Similar to Eurasian skylark, but less than 75% of its size, with wings that are 30–40% shorter and more rounded; bigger bill, shorter tail,

and proportionately longer legs; short, erectile crest. Plumage dull grayish, with buff and blackish streaks above; blackish tail has white outer feathers; legs brownish pink

**Diet:** Seeds and insects

**Breeding:** Governed by scarce, irregular rainfall; builds fragile nest of grass in small hollows under creeping vegetation or a boulder; eggs whitish, with fine grayish to brownish spots; clutch of 3 recorded. Incubation and fledging periods unknown

**Related endangered species:** Seven other species of larks are threatened, including Rudd's lark (*Heteromirafra ruddi*) CR, Ash's lark (*Mirafra ashi*) EN, and Botha's lark (*Spizocorys fringillaris*) EN

**Status:** IUCN CR; not listed by CITES

Santo Antão

São Vicente

Sal

Raso

São Nicolau

Boa Vista

**CAPE VERDE**

Maio

Brava

São Tiago

Fogo

**See also:** Climate Change **1:** 53; Fody, Mauritius **4:** 88; Rockfowl, White-Necked **8:** 38

on the nutrients provided by the guano (droppings) from seabird colonies. The bill difference enables both sexes to feed on different food items, reducing competition for the limited food supply.

Past records refer to the species as being easy to approach and showing no fear of humans, although more recent observations have suggested that the birds are now somewhat warier.

## Fluctuating Population

Censuses carried out by visiting ornithologists reveal that the Raso lark population has fluctuated over the years. Between the mid-1960s and the early 1980s estimates suggested that there were only between 20 and 50 pairs. However, a survey in early 1985 showed that there were at least 150 birds on the islet, and by 1992 the figure had risen to about 250. When a count was made in 1998, though, the researchers found a total of only 92 birds, restricted to the south and west of the islet, suggesting that the population had contracted in range and also fallen back to the alarmingly low levels found in the 1960s.

Recent droughts are almost certainly responsible for the decline. However, they indicate something other than natural climatic variability. There is evidence of long-term reversion of the land to desert in the Cape Verde Islands, probably as a result of emissions of greenhouse gases. In addition, since the lark nests on the ground, its already small population is in danger of being wiped out by rats, cats, and dogs accidentally carried to the islet by fishermen. A dog was seen on Raso in 1994, and evidence that cats were present was found during the 1998 survey. Signs of nest predation have also been found—the culprit was possibly a brown-necked raven.

Although Raso was declared a nature reserve and given legal protection in 1990, there has been no actual enforcement of protection. To ensure the survival of the Raso lark, it will be essential to check if cats or other predators have become established on the island and, if so, to eradicate them as quickly as possible. Another urgent task for conservationists is to continue to carry out regular surveys, so that they can be alerted to the first signs of further declines.

**The Raso lark** *is found on a single uninhabited island where, until recently, it has been protected by its isolation.*

# Leech, Medicinal

*Hirudo medicinalis*

*For centuries the medicinal leech was collected in Europe for its use in draining off blood, which was thought to cure many ills. Overcollection in the past and loss of habitat have now made the medicinal leech rare in western Europe.*

There are about 300 species of leech. Occurring in fresh water and on land, they breathe through their skin and have a segmented body with a sucker at each end; the sucker at the front contains the mouth. Leeches mainly feed on the blood of animals, although some aquatic leeches eat snails, insect larvae, and worms. The medicinal leech feeds on the blood of larger mammals, some amphibians, and (occasionally) fish. It sucks between two and five times its own body weight of blood at one feed and may not need to feed again for several months.

Leeches are hermaphrodites (having both male and female reproductive organs). Crossfertilization through the transfer of sperm takes place between two individuals, one acting as a male and the other as a female. The fertilized eggs are laid in cocoons and deposited on land or in water. In some species the cocoons are carried around on the underside of the parent's body for several weeks until they hatch.

Leeches swim in water by making undulations of the body. Land leeches move around in damp vegetation by looping: attaching the head sucker to the leaves, bringing up the body in a loop, attaching the rear sucker close to the head, then releasing the head, moving forward, and reattaching. They have well-developed sensory organs, including between one and four pairs of eyes and other sense receptors. The eyes respond particularly to shadows, so the vibrations caused by bigger animals moving are readily detected. Aquatic leeches can detect chemicals and scents emitted by prey in water.

Having detected the prey, leeches attach to an area of skin or enter the clothing of human victims. Then they make a Y-shaped incision with their three jaws set with sharp teeth and inject substances that anesthetize the wound, lessening the chances of detection. They also inject an anticoagulant to stop the blood from clotting and another chemical that dilates the blood vessels and increases the blood flow in the prey.

## DATA PANEL

**Medicinal leech**

*Hirudo medicinalis*

**Family:** Hirudinidae

**World population:** Unknown

**Distribution:** Asia, Europe, North America (introduced)

**Habitat:** Freshwater ponds, lakes, and marshes

**Size:** Length: up to 6 in (15 cm) when extended

**Form:** Segmented, flattened, wormlike body with front and rear suckers; tough skin, rubbery in texture

**Diet:** Blood of larger mammals, frogs, and fish

**Breeding:** Hermaphrodites (having both male and female reproductive organs) crossfertilize and lay eggs in cocoons, which are deposited on land or in water. Development does not include a larval stage

**Related endangered species:** None

**Status:** IUCN LRnt; CITES II

**See also:** Drainage and Irrigation 1: 40; Earthworm, Giant Gippsland 4: 58; Spider, Great Raft 9: 22

Being attacked by a leech carries a real risk, not so much from loss of blood (anemia) but from secondary infection of the wounds caused by blood sucking. There have also been cases of leeches entering mouths or nasal passages of animal prey and becoming so swollen with a blood meal that they blocked the breathing passages, causing the prey to suffocate. Cattle, horses, and dogs in Asia have died in this way.

## Medicinal Purposes

Centuries ago physicians prescribed blood letting (draining the blood) with leeches. During the 19th century leech treatment was used for tumors, skin diseases, gout, whooping cough, and even headaches. The practice—which did not, in fact, have a medical benefit—and the fees charged for it led to the physicians themselves being nicknamed leeches.

Although draining the blood in itself is no longer regarded as a cure, leeches do have medicinal uses. Their saliva is a source of anticoagulants for use in the prevention of blood clotting, and leeches have been used to encourage the development of the blood supply to grafts (pieces of tissue transplanted from a

**The medicinal leech** *becomes swollen after sucking blood. It can feed on up to five times its body weight of blood and can store food for several months.*

donor or a patient's own body to an area of the body needing the tissue). This is achieved by placing a leech on the graft. By drawing blood from the graft, the flow of blood into it is encouraged, and the necessary dissolved gasses and nutrients begin to reach the grafted tissue.

Ponds and marshes in the countryside used to be scoured by leech collectors, who decimated the natural population of medicinal leeches, gathering them for medicinal use. Leeching as a medical practice in Europe probably reached its peak in about the early 1800s; in 1824 five million animals were imported into the country to supplement the national stocks.

Today overcollection, together with habitat loss as a result of drainage projects and other developments, has made the medicinal leech rare. Attempts at leech farming to improve the availability of medicinal leeches have been of limited success.

# Lemur, Hairy-Eared Dwarf

### *Allocebus trichotis*

*The hairy-eared dwarf lemur is elusive and rare. It has only ever been found in a small area of eastern Madagascar known as Mananara. A concerted effort is urgently needed to safeguard its habitat and ensure its survival.*

The hairy-eared dwarf lemur is one of the world's smallest and most endangered primates. Looking more like a mouse than a monkey, it has a long, furry tail, large hands and feet, and large, beady black eyes. It is shy, nocturnal, and hardly ever comes down from the trees.

More than once the hairy-eared dwarf lemur has been believed to be extinct. Between 1875 and 1966 there were no reports of any sightings. In 1989 an expedition funded by the World Wide Fund for Nature set out to discover what had become of it. Scientists began by questioning local people living in the areas of previous sightings. Some people who had lived and worked in the forests for years claimed to have seen animals matching the description of the hairy-eared dwarf lemur. Most reports were of animals trying to escape when the trees in which they lived were chopped down. Some people admitted to having eaten dwarf lemurs that they trapped in the forest. The survey aroused the hope that this incredibly rare species survived, but also painted a grim picture of the threats facing the remaining population.

The survey also provided scientists with a lot of fresh information to help them in their hunt for living dwarf lemurs. Local people confirmed that the species was nocturnal and suggested that the animals hibernate, or at least become much less active, during the dry season. They described how the lemurs leap around on their hind legs and live in tree-holes (often in pairs), the young being born there during the wet season when food is plentiful. Armed with this new information, it was only a matter of time before the the scientists found more lemurs.

As expected, the population was extremely small, and individuals were very difficult to study in the wild. Most of what has been discovered about the species' biology has come from a study of four individuals that were caught in 1991 and kept in captivity.

Hairy-eared dwarf lemurs sleep and breed in nests made of leaves. They use their large hands to pluck

COMOROS

MADAGASCAR

MOZAMBIQUE

## DATA PANEL

**Hairy-eared dwarf lemur**

*Allocebus trichotis*

**Family:** Cheirogaleidae

**World population:** Fewer than 1,000

**Distribution:** Mananara, eastern Madagascar

**Habitat:** Lowland rain forests

**Size:** Length head/body: 5–6 in (12.5–15.2 cm); tail 6–7.5 in (14.9–19.5 cm). Weight: 2.6–3.4 oz (75–98 g)

**Form:** Tiny, dormouselike lemur with fuzzy, brownish-gray fur and a long, furry tail; eyes large and black; ears adorned with tufts of long fur

**Diet:** Large insects, fruit, and other plant material; honey

**Breeding:** Single young born in January or February after 8-week gestation. Life span unknown

**Related endangered species:** Coquerel's mouse lemur *(Mirza coquereli)* VU

**Status:** IUCN EN; CITES I

**See also:** Saving the Habitats **1:** 88; Aye-Aye **2:** 42; Lemur, Ruffed **6:** 26

**The lemur's** *name comes from* lemure, *the Latin word for ghost; it is so named because of its nocturnal habits. In the past the hairy-eared dwarf lemur was seen so rarely that it was thought to be extinct.*

flying insects from the air while hanging onto a vertical branch with their strong hind feet. They also pounce on large crickets and grab them. Unlike their close relatives, the fat-tailed mouse lemurs, dwarf lemurs do not store fat in their tail, but survive long periods of inactivity during the dry season by accumulating fat under the skin all over their body and around their intestines.

## Last Hope for the Species

All lemurs are protected by law in Madagascar; but controls are difficult to enforce, and illegal trapping continues to put the hairy-eared dwarf lemur at risk. The greatest threat to the animal, however, is the destruction of the lowland forests. Over 250,000 acres (100,000 ha) of forest were cut down between 1950 and 1985. The species' future depends on whether it can survive in regenerating woodlands or in the scraps of forest that are left.

The hairy-eared dwarf lemur is currently known to occur in three of eastern Madagascar's nature reserves, and a population has recently been discovered in rain forests at higher altitudes. It is proposed that a large area should be protected to conserve this and many other threatened species living in the forest.

The tiny populations that are known at present represent the last hope for the survival of the dwarf lemurs. However, bearing in mind the lemur's nocturnal habits and the fact that it is active for only part of the year, it is just possible that more small populations will be discovered as the Madagascan forests become better known. Thick, tropical forests are not easy to explore, and the tiny hairy-eared lemurs living in trees are hard to find.

Finally, captive breeding and releases back into the wild may also help boost numbers and increase scientific understanding of the species, just as it has for several other threatened species.

# Lemur, Philippine Flying

### Cynocephalus volans

*The Philippine flying lemur, or colugo, has been accurately described as a nonflying nonlemur; it glides rather than flies and is not a lemur! The specialized way of life of this unique creature is under threat throughout its native range.*

Although many kinds of mammal have evolved the ability to glide, few have committed themselves quite so completely to the habit as the flying lemurs or colugos of Southeast Asia. Their bodies are so specialized for gliding that they are virtually incapable of traveling in any other way. They manage to move around rather awkwardly in trees, either by dangling below the branches like sloths or gripping the trunks with their long claws and jerking their way up a few inches at a time. They never come down onto the ground if they can help it and are virtually helpless if they find themselves there. Yet high up in their rainforest home none of these apparent handicaps matter; there the flying lemur can make use of its most extraordinary attribute, the membrane or "patagium" that serves as its single wing. This parachutelike web of skin connects the animal's four limbs and tail. When it wants to move from one tree to another, it simply spread-eagles its limbs to open the patagium, taking on a kitelike appearance. It then launches itself from a trunk or branch and glides with the greatest of ease for impressive distances. Flying lemurs regularly cover 230 feet (70 m) in a single glide, and one individual has been recorded traveling an amazing 446 feet (136 m) through the air.

## Threatened Habitat

Flying lemurs put their aerial skills to good use, moving about their range at night to feed on leaves, shoots, buds, and flowers. In ideal conditions this works very well, but herein lies the flying lemur's problem. Its lifestyle is completely dependent on the availability of the right kind of habitat—namely mature tropical forest with trees whose branches start high up the trunk, so that the colugo's glide path is not obstructed, and there are clear areas of trunk on which to land. Like so many other forest animals, flying lemurs are losing habitat day by day to the timber industry and to agriculture.

Over huge areas of the colugo's former habitat natural forest has been cleared to make way for plantations. This is very damaging,

## DATA PANEL

**Philippine flying lemur (colugo)**

*Cynocephalus volans*

**Family:** Cynocephalidae

**World population:** Unknown

**Distribution:** Philippine islands of Mindanao, Basilan, Samar, Leyte, Bohol

**Habitat:** Forests dominated by trees with few lower branches

**Size:** Length head/body: 13–15 in (33–38 cm); tail: 8–11 in (22–27 cm); females are slightly larger than males. Weight: 2–3.5 lb (1–1.5 kg)

**Form:** Females have grayish fur, males slightly reddish; both have mottling on back, providing excellent camouflage on tree bark. Limbs and tail are connected by a web of skin (the patagium); fingers and toes are also webbed and bear long, curved claws.

The head is small, the face pointed, and the eyes large and round

**Diet:** Leaves, buds, flowers, and fruit of forests and plantations

**Breeding:** A single underdeveloped young is born into a fold of the tail membrane after a 2-month gestation. The longevity of flying lemurs is not known

**Related endangered species:** The Malayan colugo (*Cynocephalus variegatus*) is becoming less common, but is not currently considered at risk

**Status:** IUCN VU; not listed by CITES

Luzon
Mindoro
Palawan
Panay
Bohol
Samar
Leyte
Mindanao
Basilan
PHILIPPINES
MALAYSIA
BRUNEI
Borneo

**See also:** Specialization 1: 28; Flying Fox, Rodrigues 4: 84

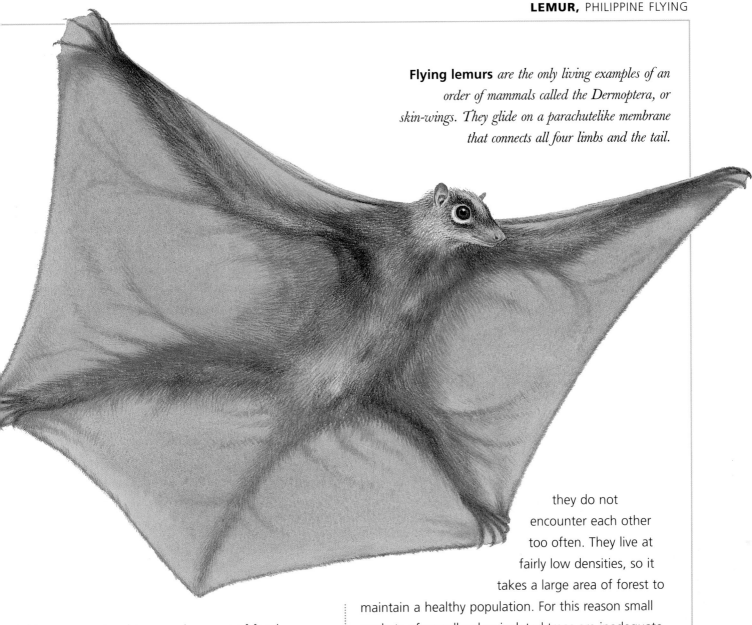

*Flying lemurs* are the only living examples of an order of mammals called the Dermoptera, or skin-wings. They glide on a parachutelike membrane that connects all four limbs and the tail.

taking away natural trees and sources of food—although plantations of rubber, with their tall, straight, evenly spaced trees, should in theory make a good replacement habitat for flying lemurs. In practice, however, plantation owners are less than happy when the nightly nibblings of the local colugo population affect their crops. The movements of flying lemurs are extremely predictable—they tend to use the same fixed routes around their range night after night—so it is a simple matter for plantation workers to catch and kill them, and many thousands of flying lemurs have been exterminated as pests.

Flying lemurs are not social animals. Often several will use the same tree, but not at the same time. Their fixed foraging routines are one way of ensuring that they do not encounter each other too often. They live at fairly low densities, so it takes a large area of forest to maintain a healthy population. For this reason small pockets of woodland or isolated trees are inadequate as alternative homes for flying lemurs.

Mothers carrying one young in their tail pouches have been found to be already pregnant with the next, so there is good reason to suppose that colugos are able to build up their numbers quite quickly if given the opportunity. Increasing population sizes is particularly urgent in the case of the Philippine flying lemur. Its Malayan relative—the only other species of flying lemur—is not currently endangered.

Ensuring the future of the Philippine flying lemur will mean designating large areas of suitable forest as sanctuaries in which logging and hunting are strictly regulated. Otherwise, the world risks losing this very special creature forever.

# Lemur, Ruffed

*Varecia variegata*

*The ruffed lemur is the largest of the true lemurs and is becoming so rare in the wild that its best hope for survival is now an intensive program of captive breeding and release.*

The ruffed lemur of Madagascar stands out among other lemurs because of its large size and distinctively patterned coat. The patterns and colors vary, but fall into two main subspecies: the red ruffed lemur and the black-and-white ruffed lemur. By far the most endangered is the red ruffed lemur, which only occurs in the far north of the species' range. Trapping and shooting are widespread activities in the area, and the local forest is being destroyed at such a rate that the IUCN predicts that unless effective action is taken, the population will plummet by at least half in the next few years.

The prospects for the black-and-white ruffed lemur are slightly brighter, although it is still a highly endangered animal. Its range is much larger than that of the red ruffed lemur, but the population is sparsely distributed. The black-and-white ruffed lemur occurs in several nature reserves, including the small island of Nosy Mangabe, where the species was introduced in the 1930s. Here the population density is much higher than elsewhere—over 30 animals per square mile (19 per sq. km). Even at these densities there are probably no more than 150 animals in total, and the population is regularly raided by poachers.

## Captive Breeding

The ruffed lemur has shown that it will take very easily to captivity, but its adaptability has been a mixed blessing. On the one hand, collecting for the Malagasy pet trade has played a large part in the species' decline. On the other, it means that there are large numbers living in the safety of zoos and conservation institutions around the world. Of the captive population, about 500 are black-and-white ruffed and 300 are red ruffed lemurs.

Over 95 percent of the population in zoos and other institutions are captive born, and there is now an extensive international breeding program, coordinated by San Diego Zoo. One problem with captive breeding is keeping the gene pool as large as possible. Although interbreeding between subspecies is strongly discouraged, there are a small number of hybrids in existence. Zoos cooperate by lending out animals for breeding so that the captive populations remain as genetically diverse as possible.

A few ruffed lemurs were successfully released back into the wild in 1998 and 1999, and at least one captive-

## DATA PANEL

**Ruffed lemur (variegated lemur)**

*Varecia variegata*

**Family:** Lemuridae

**World population:** Unknown, but probably fewer than 10,000

**Distribution:** Eastern Madagascar

**Habitat:** Rain forest from sea level to 3,900 ft (1,200 m)

**Size:** Length head/body: 20–24 in (51–60 cm); tail: 22–25 in (56–65 cm); females larger than males. Weight: 7–10 lb (3.2–4.5 kg)

**Form:** Large lemur with thick, variable coat. Black-and-white and red forms both have a white ruff, or neck patch

**Diet:** Fruit, leaves, seeds, and nectar; occasionally earth

**Breeding:** Between 2 and 6 young born after gestation of 3–3.5 months; weaned at 19 weeks; mature at 20 months; breeds before 36 months

**Related endangered species:** Golden bamboo lemur (*Hapalemur aureus*) CR; broad-nosed gentle lemur (*H. simus*) CR; 5 other members of the Lemuridae family are classified as Vulnerable

**Status:** IUCN EN; CITES I

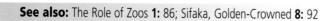

**See also:** The Role of Zoos **1:** 86; Sifaka, Golden-Crowned **8:** 92

**The ruffed lemur** *has two distinct subspecies, the red ruffed (main picture) and black-and-white ruffed (inset). Even within the two subgroups the lemurs' coat patterns are extremely variable, leading some zoologists to recommend that they are further divided into seven subspecies.*

born female has raised a family since being released back into the wild. In years to come it is hoped that the captive-bred individuals will become the founders of stable new populations in specially protected areas of the species' former range.

## Conservation Policies and Problems

Before the successful reintroduction of captive-bred lemurs can take place there needs to be a significant improvement in the way that Malagasy conservation law is enforced. Although conservation policies are in place, it is not easy for the government to make a real commitment to them in a country where the population is so poor, and where many other social and economic issues take priority. There have been instances, for example, where Malagasy nature reserves have been given up in favor of commercial logging. In addition, poaching has been allowed to continue virtually unchecked in areas that are supposedly protected.

The relatively recent development of ecotourism on Madagascar is now bringing money and trade to the island, showing both the government and local people that conservation can pay. A real change of attitude toward conservation of the island's wildlife by the local population would give the ruffed lemur a fighting chance of survival.

# Leopard

## Panthera pardus

*The adaptable leopard is a very widespread species and is still quite common in some parts of Africa. However, elsewhere hunting for fur, persecution by farmers, and loss of habitat have brought several subspecies to the brink of extinction.*

Leopards are the most adaptable of the big cats. They can live in a wide variety of climates and habitat types, so long as they have a plentiful supply of food and secure cover in which to hide their food, rear their young, and rest during the day. Prey can be anything from large antelopes and pigs to rats, rabbits, and birds, and if times are really hard, insects.

The leopard can live in forests or open spaces and at altitudes ranging from sea level to well over 16,000 feet (5,000 m). Leopards from different places often differ in appearance, none so much as the black panther, an all black or "melanistic" leopard that inhabits dark, humid forests in Southeast Asia. Regional differences are not always this obvious; but because leopards from one population are usually isolated from those elsewhere, they are recognized as distinct subspecies.

As one would expect for such a generalist predator able to cope with extremes of climate, the leopard's distribution is large. In fact, it has the widest range of any cat. Leopards once thrived in areas ranging from the baking savannas of South Africa to the lofty Himalayas, from the Javan rain forests to windswept Siberian plateaus. They are still present in these places, but in all but their African stronghold the species is in serious trouble.

Panthera pardus panthera

## DATA PANEL

**Leopard**

*Panthera pardus*

**Family:** Felidae

**World population:** Probably considerably fewer than the 700,000 estimated in 1988

**Distribution:** Largest populations in sub-Saharan Africa, with scattered and shrinking populations in northern Africa, the Middle East, Pakistan, India, Bangladesh, Sri Lanka, China, Siberia, Korea, Indochina, and Indonesia

**Habitat:** Very diverse; includes forests, grasslands, and deserts, lowlands and mountains; anywhere where there is sufficient food and cover, such as trees, scrub, or rocks

**Size:** Length head/body: 35–75 in (90–190 cm); tail 22–42 in (58–110 cm); height to shoulder: 17.5–31 in (45–78 cm); males up to 50% bigger than females. Weight: 61–200 lb (28–90 kg)

**Form:** Large, pale-buff to deep-chestnut cat marked with rosettes of dark on body and tail; head marked with smaller spots, belly and legs with large blotches; very dark or black individuals are known as black panthers

**Diet:** Mostly hoofed animals such as gazelles, wildebeest, deer, goats, and pigs, including livestock; also takes monkeys, rodents, rabbits, birds, and invertebrates

**Breeding:** Between 1 and 6 (usually 2 or 3) cubs born after gestation of 13–15 weeks at any time of year in Africa, more seasonal elsewhere; weaned at 3 months; mature at 3 years; may live over 20 years

**Related endangered species:** Asiatic lion *(Panthera leo persica)*\* CR; tiger *(P. tigris)*\* EN; snow leopard *(Uncia uncia)*\* EN; lion *(P. leo)* VU; jaguar *(P. onca)*\* LRnt

**Status:** Varies with subspecies: LR to CR. Isolated North African leopard *(Panthera pardus panthera)*, for example, is CR. All leopards CITES I

**See also:** Populations **1:** 20; Luxury Products **1:** 46; Leopard, Clouded **6:** 30

## Changing Circumstances

The problems for leopards in different parts of the species' range vary so widely that the IUCN places different regional subspecies in different categories of threat. In sub-Saharan Africa leopards are still relatively numerous, especially inside national parks such as the Serengeti. Here the protection the leopards receive and the abundant prey available to them mean that they are doing very well.

The leopard is legally protected in almost every country in its range, although several nations permit limited hunting and licenses for hunting and export of skins, and mounted trophies are granted on a regular basis. The licenses are restricted by country and usually account for between 1,000 and 2,000 leopards a year. This level of hunting is probably sustainable and an improvement on the situation in the 1960s and 1970s, when over 50,000 leopards were killed a year.

Legal hunting may not be the threat it once was, but outside protected habitats (which account for only about 13 percent of the species' range) leopards are suffering from habitat loss, persecution, and poaching. Five subspecies, from northwestern Africa, the Middle East, Siberia, and Korea are listed as Critically Endangered, with populations of fewer than 250 animals and in one case as few as 17. Four other subspecies, from the Middle East, Southeast Asia, and Indonesia are listed as Endangered.

Unlike other big cats, leopards do not seem to mind living alongside people. When areas of natural habitat are settled and turned over to agriculture, the adaptable leopard does not automatically move on. Many will stick around and adjust their behavior to make the best living they can under the circumstances. Some leopards attack livestock, and others even become man-eaters, so most governments permit the shooting of problem leopards. Man-eating leopards seem to be a particular problem in India, where dozens of people are killed by leopards every year.

**The leopard's** *coat serves to break up its outline, especially in dappled sunlight. This camouflage is useful for hunting and allows the big cat to rest undetected in the branches of a tree during the day.*

# Leopard, Clouded

### *Neofelis nebulosa*

*The clouded leopard gets its name from the cloudlike markings on its coat. The hunting of this big cat for its magnificent pelt is one of several threats to its survival.*

The clouded leopard is not actually a leopard at all. In fact, the species is sufficiently distinct to be classified all by itself. The skull and teeth of the clouded leopard are similar to those of big cats such as lions and tigers. However, it is unable to roar loudly like its large cousins, and its appearance is more like that of smaller cats, including lynx and ocelots.

The Malaysian name for the clouded leopard is *rinaudahan*, meaning tree tiger, and it is indeed one of the most accomplished feline climbers. Its broad, flexible paws grasp branches, and its long tail serves as an effective counterbalance. The clouded leopard also has remarkably flexible ankle joints—captive individuals have been observed dangling upside down from branches by just one back leg! Its arboreal skill is put to good use when hunting; the leopard will sometimes ambush unsuspecting prey by pouncing on them from above. It captures and kills monkeys and birds by knocking them off the branches of trees, just as a domestic cat swipes at smaller prey. Nevertheless, this

adaptable cat also does much of its hunting on the ground, stalking wild pigs, deer, and cattle until it is close enough to launch a sudden fatal attack.

## Starting Life

Little is known about the clouded leopard's social behavior and courtship in the wild, except that the animals appear to be solitary until the breeding season begins. Studies of individuals in zoos around the world have provided basic information about how the clouded leopard breeds. The young are born after a gestation of approximately three months. Each cub weighs 5 to 10 ounces (150 to 280 g) at birth, and its eyes remain closed for the first 10 to 12 days. The young begin to take solid food

## DATA PANEL

**Clouded leopard**

***Neofelis nebulosa***

**Family:** Felidae

**World population:** Unknown, but no more than a few thousand

**Distribution:** Asia, including Nepal, southern China, Burma, Indochina, parts of India and possibly Bangladesh, mainland Malaysia, Sumatra, Borneo and Java, Thailand, Vietnam; probably now extinct in Taiwan

**Habitat:** Dense mountain forests

**Size:** Length head/body: 28–43 in (75–110 cm); tail: 35–59 in (90–150 cm). Weight: 25–66 lb (16–30 kg)

**Form:** Large, robust-looking cat with short legs and a long tail. The yellowish coat is distinctively marked with large dark patches, each with a pale, cloudlike center. The underside, legs, and head are spotted and streaked. The eyes are yellow, and the ears are rounded

**Diet:** Deer, cattle, goats, wild pigs, monkeys, reptiles, and birds; stalked or ambushed by day and night

**Breeding:** Only observed in captivity; 1–5 (usually 2–4) young born March–August. Lives up to 17 years in captivity

**Related endangered species:** No close relatives. Taiwanese subspecies may already be extinct

**Status:** IUCN VU; CITES I

**See also:** Luxury Products **1**: 46; Cat, Iriomote **3**: 30; Lynx, Iberian **6**: 52; Ocelot, Texas **7**: 20

after 10 to 11 weeks, but the mother will continue to suckle them until they are about five months old. They are born with plenty of yellowish-gray fur marked with dark spots. The adult coat is developed at six months, and the youngsters reach independence about three months later.

## A Fragile Future

There are four geographically distinct subspecies of clouded leopard, found in Taiwan, Borneo and Malaysia, Nepal and Burma, and also China. However, there have been no recent sightings of the Taiwanese subspecies, known as the Formosan clouded leopard, and there are fears that it may already have become extinct in the wild. Elsewhere the clouded leopard survives in the most remote and undisturbed areas of mountain forests. The main problems facing the

*Clouded leopards prefer to live in dense tropical forest, where they are found at altitudes of up to 7,000 feet (2,100 m). However, they will also occupy more marginal habitats such as swampy areas and sparsely forested terrain.*

animal throughout its range are all too familiar. It is hunted for its magnificent pelt, and its teeth and bones are considered prized ingredients in traditional Eastern medicines. Erosion of the clouded leopard's habitat—as a result of deforestation by the timber industry and forest clearance for human settlement—is even more of a problem. Even when they are not being persecuted, the leopards are running out of places to live. Clouded leopards are being bred in captivity around the world, so reintroduction programs may be possible in the future, but that can only happen if areas of suitable habitat can be preserved.

# Leopard, Snow

*Uncia uncia*

*Superbly equipped for living on steep, rocky mountainsides that are blanketed with snow for much of the year, the snow leopard has evolved to cope with some of Asia's most hostile habitats. However, it is now becoming increasingly rare.*

Generally classified alongside big cats of the genus *Panthera*, the snow leopard also shares some characteristics with small cats (genus *Felis*). For example, the structure of its voice box prevents it from producing the bloodcurdling roar of a big cat, and when feeding, it adopts the crouching posture typical of a small cat.

The snow leopard's most striking features are undoubtedly its very deep fur, its long, thick, furry tail, and its big feet. All three are adaptations to living in cold conditions. The snow leopard has to contend with extremes of climate, and the thickness of the coat varies with the time of year. In winter it is up to 3 inches (8 cm) deep on the belly, but in summer it molts and becomes much finer. The long tail is also heavily furred, and the leopard uses it to cover the more exposed parts of its body when at rest. A sleeping snow leopard curls up with its tail wrapped over its nose and mouth to keep its breath from freezing.

The snow leopard has relatively large feet, but the size is exaggerated by a thick covering of fur on each paw, even on the pads. The extra fur insulates the paws against the cold ground and helps spread the leopard's weight over a larger area, allowing it to walk over snow without sinking.

Typical snow leopard habitat is steep and rocky, with dry scrub or grassland vegetation that is covered with snow for most of the winter. Prey density is usually low, so the snow leopard travels over large distances to find food, moving to different altitudes with migrating prey such as wild sheep, ibex, and musk deer. The animal's lifestyle is generally solitary,

## DATA PANEL

**Snow leopard**

*Uncia uncia*

**Family:** Felidae

**World population:** 4,500–7,400 (1992 estimate)

**Distribution:** Found in widely scattered areas in the mountains of Central Asia, from northwestern China to the Himalayas

**Habitat:** Steep, rocky mountains with dry scrub or grassland vegetation; snow-covered in winter

**Size:** Length head/body: 47–59 in (1.2–1.5 m); tail: 35 in (90 cm). Weight: male 100–165 lb (45–75 kg); female 55–110 lb (25–50 kg)

**Form:** Large, long-bodied cat with thick, creamy-gray fur marked with gray rosettes; long tail and large feet also covered in fur

**Diet:** Wild sheep, deer, gazelles, marmots, pikas, hares, gamebirds, and livestock (sheep and goats); attacks or ambushes prey at night

**Breeding:** Two or 3 cubs born in spring or early summer. Lives up to 15 years in captivity

**Related endangered species:** North African leopard (*Panthera pardus panthera*)* CR; clouded leopard (*Neofelis nebulosa*)* VU; jaguar (*P. onca*)* LRnt; other big cats

**Status:** IUCN EN; CITES I

**See also:** Biomes **1:** 18; Leopard, Clouded **6:** 30; Lynx, Iberian **6:** 52; Panther, Florida **7:** 54

though several different individuals, both male and female, may occupy much the same home range. By leaving clear scent marks or scrapes made by scratching the ground with the hind claws, neighbors warn each other of their whereabouts and avoid meeting most of the time. Males and females will join up to mate between December and March, but go their separate ways soon afterward. The female creates a cozy den, usually a rocky shelter lined with clumps of molted fur. About three and a half months after mating, she gives birth to litters of one to five (usually two or three) cubs.

## Opportunist Predators

Hunting for its winter fur has been a major factor in the snow leopard's decline. However, the international trade in skins is now banned, and the leopard has been given legal protection by the governments of the countries in which it lives. As a predator it has also suffered from a reduction in the numbers of wild mammals (such as deer, hares, and marmots) brought about by increased farming and also an upsurge in the numbers of grazing

animals such as sheep and goats. Given the opportunity, snow leopards will kill domestic animals, which leads to persecution by farmers. Nevertheless, the overall level of predation is probably not as high as local people think. A different view is taken in Tibet, where the Buddhist faith forbids the deliberate killing of any animal. Snow leopards that approach villages or farms there are usually driven away with shouts and small stones. Despite the fact that snow leopards sometimes live in close proximity to human settlements, there are no records of one ever becoming a man-eater.

**Young snow leopards** *stay with their mother for a year, during which time they learn important skills. The mother drives them away when she is ready to breed again.*

# Lion, Asiatic

### *Panthera leo persica*

*The African lion may be familiar and still relatively numerous, but the Asian subspecies is becoming scarce and is now confined to a single reserve in northwestern India.*

Lions are widespread over much of Africa south of the Sahara, but one subspecies—the Barbary lion—used to occur only in the north. The Barbary was the animal seen in Roman arenas fighting gladiators to the death. At one time the Barbary lions and their close relatives were found from northern Africa throughout the Middle East to India. All are now extinct; but a similar subspecies, the Asiatic lion, survives in the Gir Forest in northwestern India.

## A Shrinking Range

Because of the threat that lions pose to humans and livestock, they have been systematically eradicated from most of their former range. The last European lions were killed about 1,000 years ago; and once guns became widely available, they disappeared rapidly from the Middle East along with other large animals. In India British soldiers and Indian nobles hunted the Asian subspecies for sport. By 1900 only a few dozen were left; they lived in the Gir Forest, where a local prince protected them.

At that time the dry savanna and deciduous forest covered about 1,000 square miles (2,600 sq. km), but it has since shrunk to half that size. Much of what remains is now protected as a national park. The area is small, however, and is surrounded by cultivated land, so the lions are effectively marooned on a patch of suitable habitat of little more than 20 to 40 square miles (50 to 100 sq. km).

Moreover, they do not have the forest to themselves; there are several temples in the park, and five main roads and a railway track cross it. Large numbers of people are present at all times, and some have been killed by the lions; there were 81 attacks on humans, resulting in 16

---

### DATA PANEL

**Asiatic lion**

*Panthera leo persica*

**Family:** Felidae

**World population:** About 250–300

**Distribution:** Gir Forest, Gujarat State, northwestern India

**Habitat:** Dry forest and acacia savanna

**Size:** Length head/body: up to about 6.5 ft (2 m); tail: about 3 ft (1 m). Weight: male 350–420 lb (160–190 kg); female 240–260 lb (110–120 kg)

**Form:** Similar to African lion, but with thicker coat and longer tail tassel; more pronounced tuft of hair on elbows; males do not develop large mane

**Diet:** Mainly deer and medium-sized mammals

**Breeding:** Average of 2 or 3 cubs per litter born after 4-month gestation. Young take 4–8 years to reach maturity. Life span up to about 20 years

**Related endangered species:** Tiger (*Panthera tigris*)* EN; snow leopard (*Uncia uncia*)* EN

**Status:** IUCN CR; CITES I

**Female Asiatic lions** *rear their young together and suckle cubs other than their own for up to six months. The cubs start eating meat at three months.*

deaths between 1988 and 1990. To ease the problem, the sanctuary is being extended.

However, space is limited. Over 100,000 people live with their livestock within 6 miles (10 km) of the park. Domestic animals compete for food with the wild deer that the lions need as prey. When the lions go hungry, they turn to killing cattle. The government compensates local farmers for losses, but even so, lions are killed in revenge from time to time.

The cramped conditions create another danger. With the last Asiatic lions confined to one small area,

there is a risk that the entire population could be wiped out by disease. In 1994 an outbreak of distemper left scores of African lions dead in Serengeti National Park in Tanzania, eastern Africa; a similar disaster in the Gir Forest could make the Asiatic lion extinct. One solution would be to establish another population elsewhere, but in a crowded country such as India attempts to set up a lion sanctuary are often met with local resistance. One attempt to start a new population has already failed, probably as a result of illegal poisoning and shooting of the animals.

# Lizard, Blunt-Nosed Leopard

*Gambelia silus*

*The decline of this attractive lizard dates back to the California Gold Rush of 1849, when parts of its habitat were turned over to agriculture to feed the influx of miners. Since then, destruction and fragmentation of its habitat have continued.*

The habitat of the blunt-nosed leopard lizard is now restricted to a number of scattered areas in the San Joaquin Valley in California. The lizards use the deserted burrows of small mammals for shade, shelter, and hibernation in winter. Although they are diurnal (active during the day), leopard lizards tend to shelter during the hottest part of the day. They are often active at air temperatures of up to 104°F (40°C), when the soil temperature is about 122°F (50°C). From September onward the lizards take to their burrows to spend the colder months in a dormant state. Leopard lizards have predators, which is part of the natural balance; but when the lizards are forced into smaller areas by human disturbance, and their vegetation cover is destroyed, they become more exposed and vulnerable to these predators.

## The Human Threat

As the human population increased in the San Joaquin Valley, so did agriculture and urban development. This inevitably encroached on the habitat of the blunt-nosed leopard lizard. Further damage occurred as industries developed around the extraction of oil and minerals. By 1985 barely 10 percent of the original wild land on the San Joaquin Valley floor had been left undeveloped.

The road building and landfill dumping that accompanied development in the valley were also destructive to the lizard's habitat, and the damage to the delicate balance of the desert ecosystem largely ignored. Lizards and their habitats were destroyed under construction machinery; roads and irrigation ditches fragmented the lizard's territory. Pesticides sprayed on crops also had a detrimental effect on much of the wildlife. Leopard lizards are insectivorous—a large part of their diet includes insects—so their food supply can be drastically reduced, or contaminated, by the drift from crop spraying. Where the land has been adapted for pastoral farming, grazing animals eat the natural vegetation and trample rodent burrows and lizard egg

## DATA PANEL

**Blunt-nosed leopard lizard**

*Gambelia silus*

**Family:** Iguanidae

**World population:** Unknown

**Distribution:** San Joaquin Valley, California

**Habitat:** Arid areas, often alkaline, saline or sandy soils with sparse vegetation, rarely above 2,500 ft (800 m)

**Size:** Length: up to 13 in (33 cm)

**Form:** Slender lizard with long, "whippy" tail, blunt nose, and spotted throat; variable pattern of dark spots and light bars on yellow, fawn, gray, or dark-brown background; body color lightens with increased temperatures, so spots become indistinct; mated females and juveniles develop orange spots; males have red coloration in the breeding season

**Diet:** Mainly insects, other lizards, and small mammals

**Breeding:** One clutch of 2–6 eggs laid per year

**Related endangered species:** None

**Status:** IUCN EN; not listed by CITES

**See also:** Pesticides 1: 51; Iguana, Fijian Crested 5: 74; Lizard, Flat-Tailed Horned 6: 38

sites. They also break
the soil surface, which can
cause soil erosion. The removal
of natural vegetation through grazing
allows nonnative plants to invade, eliminating
the open spaces preferred by the lizard.

The threats to the blunt-nosed leopard lizard from continuing habitat destruction were highlighted as far back as 1954, but the species was not listed as endangered by the United States Department of the Interior until 13 years later. It was given state listing in 1971.

## Recovery Plans

The first recovery plan for the species was not prepared until 1980 (revised in 1985). Since then numerous studies have been carried out, including aerial surveys, to determine the amount of suitable territory still existing. Some areas have been purchased as reserves, but lack of funding has prevented this in many areas.

Conservation is a complex business needing comprehensive studies of numerous aspects: ecology, population, feeding habits, breeding, and genetic variability. Although much information has now been gathered, the scattered nature of the remaining lizard sites complicates matters because of environmental

**The blunt-nosed leopard lizard** *is active by day and prefers hot, dry, and sparsely vegetated areas. It can run on its hindlegs to escape predators, which include snakes, birds, and mammals.*

variation. It may be a long time before all the necessary knowledge is accumulated.

The blunt-nosed leopard lizard has proved itself to be adaptable, often colonizing sites that have been disturbed then abandoned. However, unless the decline of its habitat and its continued isolation in ever-shrinking areas are halted, the species may never recover. Its survival depends on further land acquisition and the construction of "corridors" to allow groups to move between fragmented sites, so preventing the genetic problems that develop in small populations. Its habitat must be protected, improved, and managed in such a way that the land is only used in a manner compatible with the lizard's existence. This is a tall order given the conflicting interests over land use. Recovery of this species will take a very long time; it remains to be seen if it will be successful.

# Lizard, Flat-Tailed Horned

*Phrynosoma m'callii*

*Originally mistaken for toads by the early American settlers, the flat-tailed horned lizards have long been popular pets and in many areas were collected and sold in their thousands.*

Horned lizards were highly regarded by early cultures in the southwestern United States and Mexico; the few species of horned lizard that squirt blood from their eyes when disturbed were particularly intriguing to people. Images of lizards feature on many artifacts found in the area. The settlers originally thought that the lizards were toads because of their squat shape and toadlike head. Their scientific name, *Phrynosoma,* comes from the Greek words *phryno,* meaning toad, and *soma,* meaning body. In many areas the lizards were collected and sold in their thousands as pets, but the trade is now illegal in most states.

There are about 15 species of horned lizard that inhabit desert, semidesert, and the open forest in the United States. The flat-tailed species is limited to a fairly small area, much of which is being systematically destroyed. It has survived for millions of years in harsh desert areas, where temperatures can reach over 110°F (43°C). The species was discovered by and named after Colonel George M'Call in 1852. All *Phrynosoma* species look similar; the flat-tailed horned lizard fits the general description but has a flattened tail that is longer than usual. Their coloring provides excellent camouflage in their sandy habitat. Although they can move quickly, they rely on their flattened body merging with the background and often bury themselves in loose sand. Compared to some *Phrynosoma* species, the flat-tailed lizard has a relatively low reproduction rate. Other *Phrynosoma* lizards are known to produce 25 eggs or more; some living at high altitudes bear live young.

## Threat to Habitat and Range

Like many other species, the flat-tailed horned lizard is now threatened with extinction because of human activity. It was classed as Sensitive in 1980 by the Bureau of Land Management; in 1993 the United States Fish and Wildlife Service (USFWS) proposed changing the listing to Threatened under the Endangered Species Act (ESA). The matter was unresolved until conservation groups took legal action. In response, the USFWS withdrew the proposal and instead issued a habitat conservation plan and management strategy. The judge ruled that the plan was sufficient and that further protection under the ESA was not necessary. The conservationists have appealed.

The range of the flat-tailed horned lizard once extended farther than today, but fragmentation and destruction of its habitat over many years have gradually squeezed it into a

## DATA PANEL

**Flat-tailed horned lizard**

*Phrynosoma m'callii*

**Family:** Iguanidae

**World population:** Unknown

**Distribution:** Southeastern California; southwestern Arizona into northern Sonora; Mexico; Baja California

**Habitat:** Arid desert scrubland

**Size:** Length: 4–5 in (11–13 cm)

**Form:** Flattened body; short spines and tubercules (domelike projections) on back; 1 or 2 fringes of short, pointed scales along each side; spiny horns on head. Coloration pale gray, reddish brown, buff, and dark brown

**Diet:** Mainly ants; also other insects

**Breeding:** Between 3 and 7 eggs laid; possibly more than 1 clutch per year

**Related endangered species:** Many members of the family Iguanidae

**Status:** IUCN LRcd; not listed by CITES

**See also:** Organizations **1:** 10; Habitat Loss **1:** 38; Lizard, Blunt-Nosed Leopard **6:** 36

smaller area that is still being destroyed. Closely dependent on its habitat of loose sand, and well adapted to the prevailing harsh climatic conditions, it is highly vulnerable to the degradation of its territory. One large-scale loss of habitat occurred early in the 20th century when over 300,000 acres (121,410 ha) were flooded by water from the Colorado river to form the Salton Sea. Over the past 30 to 40 years about 50 percent of the flat-tailed lizard's habitat has been destroyed by agriculture and urban development. Current studies indicate that the rest of its territory will also disappear unless preventive measures are taken.

Large areas have been converted for crops, and the construction of irrigation ditches has fragmented the lizard's range. With agriculture come pesticides, which destroy the ants and other insects on which the lizards feed, as well as killing the lizards themselves. Introduced plants also alter the habitat so that it is no longer suitable for the creatures it once sustained. Urban development brings with it roads, which are responsible for a significant number of lizard deaths. A reptile regulates its body temperature by basking in the sun. A warm road surface offers ideal basking conditions—with fatal results. In addition, the spread of housing brings predators in the form of domestic pets. Other animals are attracted by trash dumps. New features of the landscape such as fences, telegraph poles, and pylons provide vantage points for predators such as ravens and jays.

As human settlements spread farther into the desert, more areas are used for recreational activities, particularly those involving off-road vehicles. Such activities threaten the desert ecosystem in many areas, destroying the vegetation, disturbing lizards' nests, and even killing the lizards. Destruction of vegetation causes soil erosion, ruining the habitat for a whole community of desert animals. Off-road vehicle activity could easily be prevented or reduced by legislation, but no legal measures have yet been introduced.

Flat-tailed horned lizards are not entirely unprotected; their collection and sale without a special permit is banned. However, some people ignore the regulations and risk prosecution.

**The flat-tailed horned lizard** *has many useful characteristics: Its platelike scales reduce water loss; its sharp spines deter attackers; and its long legs are useful for clambering over branches.*

39

# Lizard, Ibiza Wall

## Podarcis pityusensis

*The colorful appearance of this lizard has made it popular among hobbyists and consequently a frequent victim of illicit trade. It is also vulnerable to the effects of tourism on its environment.*

Although the Ibiza wall lizard takes its name from Ibiza, the main island in the Balearics, it is also found on numerous smaller islands, some of them little more than rocky islets with hardly any vegetation. It is quite adaptable, often found near human habitation in stone walls and ruined buildings, but also existing in scrubland and quite barren areas, even on steep cliffs.

The shape and coloration of the lizard vary from island to island. This variation has been a source of interest to scientists, and over 40 different subspecies of *Podarcis pityusensis* have been named. However, not all zoologists recognize subspecies, preferring to call them "geographical variations" or "races" of the same animal. In some cases the situation has been confused by the construction of causeways linking islands. Fishermen have also collected particularly colorful lizards from one island and released them on another nearer home so that they can be collected and sold if the opportunity arises. This has led to some interbreeding between different "races," making study difficult.

The Ibiza wall lizard is an attractive creature, and reptile-keeping hobbyists have been eager to add it to their collections. Collectors ranged from vacationers who took home a few specimens or reptile enthusiasts who took some for themselves and some to sell, to those operating on a commercial scale. Seizures by customs have included 2,000 lizards at Schipol Airport, the Netherlands, and two seizures of 500 and 400 lizards found packed in suitcases at Heathrow Airport, England. Out of the batch of 500 only 80 lizards survived their trauma to be flown back to the Balearic Islands. No doubt other batches have got through undetected. Under Spanish law collecting lizards is illegal, but the law is not always rigorously enforced.

The main source of income on the Balearic Islands used to be agriculture: Olive groves, grapes,

---

## DATA PANEL

**Ibiza wall lizard**

*Podarcis pityusensis*

**Family:** Lacertidae

**World population:** Unknown

**Distribution:** Balearic Islands, Spain

**Habitat:** Dry, rocky areas with some plant cover; sometimes found in stone walls and ruined buildings

**Size:** Length: varies from island to island, but on average 6–8 in (15–20 cm)

**Form:** Color and shape vary from island to island. "Large island" populations generally green on back, sometimes brown or gray, light lines along sides interspersed with spots or streaks; "small island" populations are sometimes melanistic—lack light pigments—tending to be black, dark brown, or dark blue, often with a dorsal pattern; some have blue or orange areas on flanks

**Diet:** Mainly insects, some small invertebrates; sometimes young geckos or their own young; occasionally fruit, berries, and nectar

**Breeding:** Possibly 2 clutches per year of 2–6 eggs

**Related endangered species:** Lilford's wall lizard (*Podarcis lilfordi*) VU; Miles wall lizard (*P. milensis*) VU

**Status:** IUCN VU; CITES II

SPAIN

Majorca    Minorca

Ibiza    Balearic Islands

Formentera

ALGERIA

---

**See also:** Tourism 1: 42; Exploitation of Live Animals 1: 49; Lizard, Sand 6: 42

**Lizard populations** *in the Balearic Islands have evolved in isolation as rising waters of the Mediterranean Sea have cut off the islands from the mainland.*

almonds, and citrus fruit were the main crops. The 1960s saw a rapid increase in tourism, which brought large amounts of money to the islands. The warm climate, sandy beaches, and attractive scenery continue to draw thousands of tourists every year. Tourism now accounts for 80 percent of the islands' income; many local people have stopped farming and gained jobs connected with tourism.

**Habitats under Threat**

The growth of tourism has destroyed much of the lizards' former habitat. Land has been leveled to build hotels, golf courses, shops, parks, and various other tourist amenities. One islet was dynamited to improve navigation. Many of the small islets are visited by tourists who clamber about, unaware that they may be destroying lizards' nests and the vegetation.

In several Mediterranean holiday resorts, including the Balearics, deliberate eradication, including poisoning lizards around hotels, has taken place to prevent them from scaring the visitors. Although killing the lizards is illegal, it is difficult to stop. Space is at a premium in the Balearics, and setting up "biogenetic reserves," as recommended under the 1979 Berne Convention on the Conservation of European Wildlife and Natural Habitats, is difficult.

The Balearic government has researched the ecology of the lizards, but deciding which of the different forms should be protected is difficult. Saving every different island population is impossible, and some will no doubt eventually disappear. Some of the islands are also home to rare plants, birds, and seals, so establishing protected reserves would benefit more than just the lizards.

Apart from some local restrictions placed on urban and tourist developments, the situation remains largely unchanged. Further problems will inevitably arise as the lucrative tourist industry grows.

# Lizard, Sand

*Lacerta agilis*

*In Britain, where all native species of lizard and snake are threatened, the sand lizard is among the most endangered. It has a restricted range and is totally dependent on a specific type of habitat. In mainland Europe the species seems to be more adaptable.*

In its northern range the sand lizard is a lowland species, restricted to coastal sand dunes that offer some plant cover and sandy heathlands where heather proliferates. In Britain the lizards are confined mainly to the sand dunes of the Merseyside coast in northwestern England and the sandy heathlands of Dorset and Hampshire on the English south coast.

## Shrinking Habitat

Sand lizard sites have been declining in Northern Europe since the late 19th century. In many cases the lizard's habitat has been invaded and altered by plants such as birch, pines, gorse, and bracken. However, the major threat has come from human activity. Both the Merseyside coast and the Dorset and Hampshire downs are popular with tourists. Although some areas are protected reserves administered by a variety of organizations, the land outside the reserves is subject to great pressure. Walkers unknowingly compact egg sites and generally disrupt the lizard's habitat. In addition, much of the range has been disturbed by new housing developments. As well as being preyed on by foxes and hedgehogs—the sand lizard's major natural predators—the species is now also at risk from domestic cats and dogs.

Although the Dorset heaths are designated Sites of Special Scientific Interest, the need for urban development seems to have overridden all other considerations. Sand and gravel extraction for the construction industry have also destroyed a number of habitats along the south coast. Once the natural vegetation disappears, the area is invaded by grasses, bracken, gorse, and other plants that make the area unsuitable for sand lizards. Heath fires are a serious problem.

## DATA PANEL

**Sand lizard**

*Lacerta agilis*

**Family:** Lacertidae

**World population:** Unknown

**Distribution:** Northern Europe, including Britain, France, Italy, south Balkans, and Iberia west to Central Asia

**Habitat:** Dry, sandy dunes; heaths

**Size:** Length head/body: up to 8 in (20 cm); tail: 8–14 in (20–30 cm)

**Form:** Small, robust, stout-bodied lizard. Distinct band of narrow scales runs along back. Coloration and pattern variable; Male has green along sides (vivid in spring). Dark broken stripe, bordered by 2 lighter stripes, runs along back. Female has dark blotches on gray to brown background. Underside of male is yellow-green with small, dark spots; female white to pale yellow without spots. Long, clawed digits

**Diet:** Insects; occasionally fruit

**Breeding:** One clutch of 5–14 eggs

**Related endangered species:** *Lacerta bonnali* (no common name) VU; Soutpansberg rock lizard (*L. rupicola*) LRnt; Schreiber's green lizard (*L. schreiberi*) LRnt; *L. vivipara pannonica* (no common name) VU

**Status:** Not listed by IUCN; not listed by CITES

42

EX EW CR EN VU LR O

REPTILE

**See also:** Education **1:** 94; Lizard, Ibiza Wall **6:** 40

Since the overstretched fire service has to make property protection its first priority, heath fires sometimes go unattended.

Fires, road construction, and mineral extraction not only destroy habitats, but also fragment them. As a result, lizard populations are confined to ever smaller areas where they are at greater risk of predation. Inbreeding is also more likely in small, isolated populations, leading to genetic weaknesses.

Sand lizards are a gregarious species, although fighting occurs among males in spring. They often dig holes and also make use of burrows made by small mammals. Eggs are buried in sandy, south-facing slopes and left to hatch. Adult lizards are said to eat hatchlings, which reduces numbers and can be a problem in small ranges. The young are unable to disperse to an area in which they are not in competition with their parents and therefore run more risk of being eaten.

## Conservation Efforts

Several conservation agencies are working toward reversing the decline in sand-lizard numbers. Ecological studies of the species exploring their requirements have been carried out. In several reserves scrub has been cleared from the lizards' habitat and other improvements made. Under the Species Recovery Plan captive-breeding programs have been set up in zoos or with private breeders, and sand lizards have been reintroduced to sites that still provide a suitable habitat. In 1970, 51 lizards were released on the Island of Coll off the west coast of Scotland, but their progress has not been monitored.

Sand lizards from different areas may display different coloration and also genetic variations. Populations are therefore kept separate to help ensure the breeding of healthy specimens.

However, the Species Recovery Plan will not be effective until the regulations protecting sand-lizard habitat drawn up by the Berne Convention and the Wildlife and Countryside Act are applied more rigorously. Conservation agencies are trying to persuade the authorities to make greater efforts, but in some cases lack of resources is a problem. More money, for example, could pay for extra wardens to patrol and protect the reserves. Although education programs exist, convincing people that lizards and snakes are worth saving is often a difficult task.

**The female sand lizard** *is grayish brown with long, clawed digits that help it cling to rocks.*

# Longicorn, Cerambyx

### Cerambyx cerdo

*Longhorn beetles originate mainly in the tropics, but the international trade in timber has introduced many species to temperate countries. The cerambyx longicorn beetle has managed to survive in northern Europe, but it is now rare.*

Longhorn beetles have long, narrow bodies with attractive and sometimes colorful markings—especially on their wing cases. They are sometimes called timber beetles because their larvae or grubs feed on and develop in timber. Longhorn beetles include the old house borer commonly found in roof timbers. The worldwide timber trade has widened the distribution of longhorn beetles. Timber imports have established isolated populations of about 70 species in northern Europe, but some, like the cerambyx longicorn, are barely managing to hold on in their new homelands and consequently are rare.

Adult cerambyx longicorns are typically beetle-shaped, with colorful markings and long, threadlike antennae that can be folded back along the body in flight. In some longhorn beetle species the eyes have notches into which the antennae can fold. The antennae normally measure at least two-thirds of the beetle's total length, but may be longer. In the case of the cerambyx longicorn beetle the antennae are very long and reach back well beyond the tail.

### Life Stages of Longhorn Beetles

As is so often the case with insects, the adults have a very different lifestyle from the larvae. The adults of many longhorn beetle species feed on nectar, visiting a variety of woodland flowers, but some eat the leaves of the trees in which their larvae develop.

The males of some species are quite ferocious. If disturbed while at rest or while mating, they can make loud "warning" sounds by rubbing or rasping two parts of the thorax against each other. Production of sounds in this way is known as stridulation. The males are known to fight with other males of the same species and may end up biting off parts of their antennae or legs.

After mating the female longhorn beetle seeks out deep cracks or fissures in the bark of trees in which to

## DATA PANEL

**Cerambyx longicorn**

**Cerambyx cerdo**

**Family:** Cerambycidae

**World population:** Unknown

**Distribution:** Northern Europe, including Britain, Spain, and Sweden; Ukraine; northern Africa, including Algeria, Morocco, and Tunisia

**Habitat:** Adults live among temperate woodland plants, while larvae prefer rotting and stored timber

**Size:** Length: up to 1.2 in (3 cm); antennae: up to 1.4 in (3.6 cm)

**Form:** Adult: slender, oblong beetle, with long, threadlike antennae; color drab, but has reddish tips to its wing cases. Larva: pale grub

**Diet:** Adults feed on nectar or leaves of host trees. Larvae eat rotting or dry wood, such as roof timbers

**Breeding:** Female lays eggs deep in bark of tree. Eggs hatch into larvae after about 3 weeks. Larvae may pass several years in timber before they pupate and emerge as adults

**Related endangered species:** Rosalia longicorn (*Rosalia alpina*) VU

**Status:** IUCN VU; not listed by CITES

**See also:** Specialization 1: 28; Introductions 1: 54; Beetle, Blue Ground 2: 78; Beetle, Hermit 2: 80

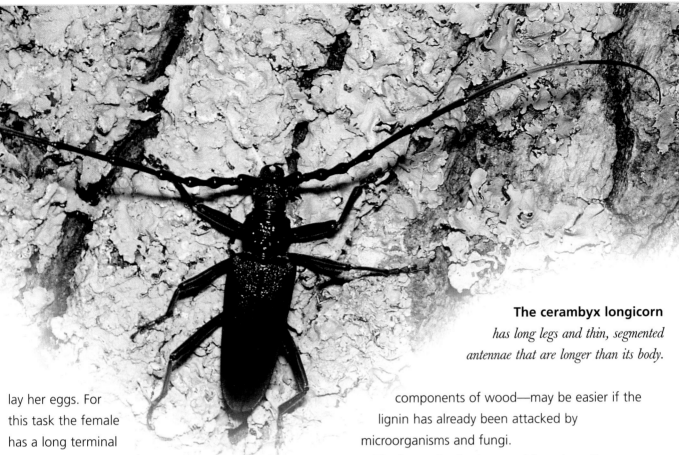

**The cerambyx longicorn**
*has long legs and thin, segmented*
*antennae that are longer than its body.*

lay her eggs. For this task the female has a long terminal ovipositor formed from the last few segments of the abdomen. This tubular structure is retractile and is ideal for depositing the eggs deep inside the timber. The deposited eggs hatch after about three weeks into whitish, round larvae.

The head of the larva is armed with strong jaws, which enable it to eat its way through wood, both live and dead, leaving large bore holes in the tree as it goes. Biting into wood requires exceptionally strong jaws, and the larva's jaws are reinforced with a substance called sclerotin (made mainly from chitin—the main component of the insect exoskeleton—protein, and waxes or calcium salts). This makes the jaws so strong that wood-boring beetle larvae have been shown to be able to bite through sheets of lead, silver, copper, and zinc! Longhorn beetle larvae are also remarkable because they can digest cellulose, the material that forms the cell walls of plants. Very few animals can do this. The longhorn larvae succeed because their digestive juices contain an enzyme that helps in the breakdown of cellulose into digestible components. Feeding on cellulose and lignin—the

components of wood—may be easier if the lignin has already been attacked by microorganisms and fungi.

The larvae live in the wood for a long time, possibly up to four years. Eventually, they move toward the outside surface of the bark and make a cell in which to pupate. After pupation an adult beetle emerges. There are some tales of longhorn beetles emerging from furniture and pit-props some 20 years after they were made. Although it is difficult to gauge the truth of such stories, they are not implausible. They illustrate the time that some species of longhorn beetle take to pass through their larval development. The American longhorn beetle *Eburia quadrigeminata* has been recorded as living in timber for 40 years!

## Conservation

Longhorn beetles provide a good example of the way in which people can accidentally disturb the natural distribution of organisms by trade and traffic. Conservation of some longhorn beetle species may be a complex operation, but the provision of host plants for the adults and larvae is likely to be a worthwhile exercise and has shown great benefits for other endangered insect species such as butterflies.

# Loris, Slender

## *Loris tardigradus*

*The slender loris was first described when Dutch explorers brought captured specimens back from India. People were delighted by the little primate's comical expression and its habit of swaying from side to side, attributes that earned it the Dutch name "loris," meaning clown.*

The slender loris of Sri Lanka and India is the mammalian equivalent of the chameleon. Its woolly, gray fur is not true camouflage, but its dull color enables the loris to make itself virtually invisible as it hunts for insect prey high in the trees. It moves so slowly and smoothly that it can pass virtually unnoticed. Like a chameleon, it also has long legs and specialized gripping feet with opposing digits.

Remaining undiscovered is the species' best defense against predators; a loris can stay absolutely motionless for hours, long enough for any casual observer to get bored and move on. If the predator continues to approach, the loris has further defensive tricks up its furry sleeve. It will glare at the intruder while growling threateningly and release an unpleasant smell from a special gland. As a last resort the loris will let go of its branch and drop onto a lower one, or to the ground, where it will scamper away quickly.

## Threats to the Habitat

The stealthy concealment used by the slender loris only works well in dense vegetation. Although lorises can survive successfully in various different kinds of forest, the foliage must be lush enough to provide good cover. As forests are destroyed for timber or to make way for agriculture, the loris is increasingly at risk.

Lorises will move into areas of scrubby and regenerating woodland, but only if it is adjacent to untouched habitat since they prefer not to travel across open ground. Consequently, isolated areas of suitable forest remain unoccupied since lorises will not migrate into them. In addition, if a small patch of loris habitat is cut off by tree-felling or development, the resident population is trapped and cannot expand. The animals soon die out, as inbreeding, lack of space, and local threats such as fire, disease, or hunting take their toll.

Hunting is not a major danger, but a significant number of lorises are undoubtedly killed for their body parts, which are used in traditional medicine.

## Conservation Issues

Endearing though it appears, the slender loris does not make a good pet

---

### DATA PANEL

**Slender loris**

*Loris tardigradus*

**Family:** Lorisidae

**World population:** Unknown

**Distribution:** India and Sri Lanka

**Habitat:** Varies from rain forest to dry, swampy, or scrubby deciduous forests. Wide range of altitudes

**Size:** Length: 6–10 in (16–26 cm). Weight: 3–12.5 oz (85–350 g)

**Form:** Slender-limbed, tailless primate with short, woolly gray fur. Face dominated by large, round, forward-facing eyes encircled by dark patches; rounded ears; pink nose. Large thumbs and toes oppose other digits to form powerful pincers for gripping branches

**Diet:** Fruit, leaves, shoots, flowers, and insects; occasionally birds' eggs and small vertebrates

**Breeding:** One or 2 young born April–May or October–November after 6-month gestation; weaned at 2–7 months. Males mature at 18 months, females at 10 months. Life span up to 15 years

**Related endangered species:** Pygmy loris (*Nycticebus pygmaeus*)—one of the two species of slow lorises—VU

**Status:** IUCN EN (3 subspecies, under debate as to their taxonomic definition, are EN; 2 are DD); CITES II

INDIA

SRI LANKA

---

**See also:** Populations **1:** 20; Speciation **1:** 26; Island Biogeography **1:** 30; Lemur, Ruffed **6:** 26

**The slender loris** *is arboreal and nocturnal. It uses its slender limbs and gripping feet to move around in the trees. The related slow lorises are slower moving and are found in Southeast Asia and the Malay Peninsula.*

and does not take well to life in captivity. In the wild lorises live alone and are fiercely territorial, vigorously scent-marking their domains. In captivity they are notoriously bad-tempered and aggressive. Noisy and often fatal fights break out when lorises are kept close to each other.

Early attempts at captive breeding of slender lorises were disappointing. Even in the wild, lorises are slow breeders, usually only giving birth to single young and breeding just once a year.

Another problem for conservationists is that no one is sure how many slender loris species exist. There are three distinct types of slender loris living in Sri Lanka, and some scientists think that they are different enough to be classed as three separate species. When the different types were brought together in a captive-breeding program, the attempt was unsuccessful, adding weight to the separate species claim. However, taking into account their dislike of captivity, the failure of the group to breed could just as easily have been caused by stress.

At present the slender loris does not receive any protection except where it lives within national parks and nature reserves. However, the animal is still at risk, and it is therefore important that the fortunes of the world's wild populations are closely monitored so that appropriate steps can be taken should their situation get worse.

# Lovebird, Black-Cheeked

*Agapornis nigrigenis*

*The black-cheeked lovebird is a little parrot that occupies a restricted range in southwestern Zambia, Central Africa. The causes of its continuing decline are not yet fully understood.*

The black-cheeked lovebird is one of a group of closely related species of parrot. Apart from one species that is found on Madagascar and nearby Indian Ocean islands, all lovebirds are found in continental Africa. Lovebird pairs preen one another with their bills. It is this habit that gives these birds their common name. Pairs of birds mate for life.

The total range of the black-cheeked lovebird may be as little as 1,760 square miles (4,550 sq. km) in southwestern Zambia, extending from the Zambezi River on the country's southern border with Zimbabwe to the Kafue River farther north. There are two subpopulations, with about 3,800 birds in the north (including those living in the Kafue National Park in the extreme north of the range) and about 6,200 birds in the south. In the past a few birds have been seen in the extreme north of Zimbabwe at Victoria Falls, and they may still occur elsewhere in small patches, although these records may refer to feral birds.

The birds spend the dry season within a core area of only about 960 square miles (2,500 sq. km) of woodland along the rivers. When the crops ripen during the wet season, they move into the fields to feast on sorghum and millet grains.

## Bird Trade

Huge numbers of black-cheeked lovebirds were trapped for the international cage-bird trade during the 1920s. At the peak of the trade in 1929, 16,000 of the parrots were trapped in just a month; today the entire population is thought to be only about 10,000. Although the export of black-cheeked lovebirds from Zambia was banned from 1930 onward, it is likely that the trade in trapped birds continued until the 1960s.

## Current Threats

No one knows the reasons for the continued decline in numbers of the lovebirds. Trapping for the cage-bird trade reportedly continues, at least for local markets, and there is always a possibility that more serious exploitation will be revived. In 1992, 170 wild individuals were recorded in international trade, but there is no evidence that trapping on a large scale has resumed. In some places black-cheeked lovebirds are killed because they damage crops.

## DATA PANEL

**Black-cheeked lovebird (black-faced lovebird)**

*Agapornis nigrigenis*

**Family:** Psittacidae

**World population:** About 10,000 individuals

**Distribution:** Small area in southwestern Zambia; possibly occurs in a few places elsewhere, including a small area of Namibia

**Habitat:** Mopane and acacia woodlands (lowland plains with woodland dominated by the plants *Colophospermum mopane* and *Acacia* species) in river valleys

**Size:** Length: 5–5.5 in (13–14 cm). Weight (captive birds): up to 1.5 oz (43 g)

**Form:** Small, stocky parrot with large head and bill and short, rounded tail; mainly green plumage, darker above and paler beneath; blackish-brown hood, ocher-yellow nape, rusty-orange patch on upper breast, and green rump distinguishes the species from other lovebirds; bill coral red; white ring around each eye

**Diet:** Small seeds of wild grasses and other plants and grain; flowers, buds, and berries

**Breeding:** January–April. Nests in holes in mature mopane trees; 3–8 white eggs laid; incubation period about 3.5 weeks; fledging about 6 weeks

**Related endangered species:** Fischer's lovebird *(Agapornis fischeri)* LRnt

**Status:** IUCN VU; CITES II

DEMOCRATIC REPUBLIC OF CONGO
ANGOLA
ZAMBIA
ZIMBABWE
NAMIBIA
BOTSWANA

**See also:** Exploitation of Live Animals **1:** 49; Macaw, Spix's **6:** 60

Another suggested cause of the decline of the species is that individuals may have interbred with the Nyasa (or Lilian's) lovebird. The two species are so closely related that they were previously regarded as merely geographical races of the same species. They are separated by the 60 miles (100 km) or so of gorges below Victoria Falls and about 90 miles (150 km) of what is locally called miombo woodland in the Zambezi Valley, an area that is ecologically unsuitable and thus avoided by both species. However, hybridization may still be possible between the wild black-cheeked species and feral Nyasa lovebirds. However, this is now thought to be unlikely.

A change in farming methods is much more likely to have caused declines. Between the 1930s and 1950s farmers in many areas stopped growing sorghum and millet, switching to corn, whose larger seeds the parrots do not eat.

The main threat to the birds today, however, may well be the increasing incidence of drought, possibly due to long-term climate changes. Drought deprives the lovebirds of drinking water—they probably need to drink every day, and they are particular about the source of water. In the absence of suitable water they may have deserted affected areas.

## Conservation

The Research Center for African Parrot Conservation at the University of Natal in eastern South Africa has begun a project to obtain information about the threats facing the species and its precise ecological requirements so that an effective conservation plan can be prepared.

Investigating the little-known breeding ecology of the black-cheeked lovebird may reveal why it has so far failed to recover its numbers. Even in areas where sorghum and millet are available and there is no trapping, numbers have not always increased. The inability to recover is puzzling, especially since other lovebird species can breed rapidly if conditions are favorable.

The project is making a survey throughout the entire historical range of the bird, as well as a more intensive population study within a selected area. A vital element is the involvement of local people, and running alongside the research is an awareness program about conservation of the species. The project is the first stage in saving the black-cheeked lovebird from continued decline.

**The black-cheeked lovebird** *is the size of a plump sparrow. An orange patch on the upper breast is one of the factors that distinguishes the species from other lovebirds.*

49

# Lungfish, Australian

*Neoceratodus forsteri*

*Fish breathe through their gills; land-based animals use their lungs. However, the division is not as clearcut as it might appear. Some can use other parts of the body for respiration as well, such as a special organ in the gill chamber, parts of the gut, or (like the Australian lungfish) a lung.*

The Australian lungfish, along with its closest relatives, the African and South American lungfish, is regarded as a primitive animal: There is even some doubt as to whether it is really a fish at all. Evidence includes the fact that some species have characteristics that indicate similarities with amphibians. They include external gills during the larval stages, limblike pectoral and pelvic fins, the continuous dorsal (back), caudal (tail), and anal (belly) fins, the large heavy-duty body scales, and lungs.

## Australian Differences

The Australian, or Queensland, lungfish, while sharing many characteristics with its African and South American cousins, differs from them in significant ways. The most fishlike of all the species, its fins look more like fins than underdeveloped legs. Its newly hatched larvae also lack the amphibianlike external gills present in the young of other species, although at first they still look more like tadpoles than baby fish.

One important difference relates to the lungs. Other lungfish have two such structures consisting of extensions of the esophagus (gullet) that run along the top of the abdominal cavity, roughly in the same position as the swim-bladder in "normal" fish. In the Australian lungfish, while the arrangement is similar, there is only one lung.

Another difference relates to summer survival. All lungfish are able to supplement their gill breathing by taking atmospheric air into their lungs at the water surface. They are also capable of tolerating unfavorable (oxygen-deficient) water conditions that would kill most other fish. In the African and South American species this survival capacity is taken a step further. Not only can the lungfish survive very low-oxygen water conditions, they can even survive periods of drought when the pools in which they live dry out completely.

As the drying out process goes on, the fish burrow into the bottom mud, secrete a mucous "cocoon" or chamber (the South American lungfish does not line its chamber with mucus), and go into a state of estivation (dormancy) until the arrival of the next rains. The Australian lungfish does not have this ability and will die if its native waters dry out. Nevertheless, its survival capabilities are resilient enough to allow at least some individuals to survive a few days out of water as long as they are in the shade, and their body remains moist.

## Ancient Lineage

The history of lungfish can be traced back through the fossil record. Fossils of the Australian type of lungfish have been found in Triassic rocks (about 203 million years old). Fossil cocoons, or burrows—sometimes with a lungfish inside—have been found in Permian and Carboniferous rocks (270 and 350 million years old, respectively). However, the heyday of lungfish appears to have been during the Devonian period—from about 350 to 400 million years ago. Fossils of lungfish that are apparently identical to modern-day Australian lungfish have been found in rocks about 100 million years old in New South Wales. The Australian lungfish is recognized as the oldest known species of fish today. Consequently, it enjoys the status of "living fossil."

**See also:** Specialization **1:** 28; What Is a Fish? **1:** 68; Coelacanth **3:** 58; Frog, Tinkling **5:** 12; Paradisefish, Ornate **7:** 56

**Australian lungfish** *have an ancient lineage that can be traced through the fossil record over millions of years.*

## Threatened or Not?

Undoubtedly, all lungfish are fascinating from the biological point of view, and the Australian lungfish is no exception. It has therefore been studied in great detail, and its distribution is well documented. We know as a result of these studies that lungfish were once widely distributed throughout Australia. Today, however, the species is only found naturally in southeastern Queensland, within the Burnett and Mary river systems. Over the years it has also been introduced into other southeastern Queensland waters, some of which are now known to hold self-sustaining populations.

While this restricted distribution may appear to justify concern about the ongoing survival of the species, informed opinion seems to be reasonably confident that the Australian lungfish is no longer heading for extinction. Today, probably as a result of the protection it receives, populations are on the increase, which bodes well for its future.

### DATA PANEL

**Australian lungfish**

*Neoceratodus forsteri*

**Family:** Ceratodidae

**World population:** Numbers believed to be relatively high within the range. Some introduced populations are self-sustaining

**Distribution:** Naturally occurring in the Mary and Burnett river systems of southeastern Queensland, Australia. Introduced into other watercourses and into some reservoirs in Queensland and northern New South Wales

**Habitat:** Still pools or other bodies of deep, slow-flowing water, which are susceptible to seasonal fluctuations in water level, clarity, and quality

**Size:** Length: up to 5 ft (1.5 m). Weight: 88 lb (40 kg)

**Form:** Sturdy, but elongated body; paddlelike pectoral (chest) and pelvic (hip) fins. Dorsal (back), caudal (tail), and anal (belly) fins are continuous. Body scales are stout, large, round, and

overlapping. Eyes are small in relation to body. Coloration olive-green or gray-brown on back and down sides, but white on underside of head and along belly; scattering of dark irregular spots adorns side of body in many specimens, increasing in abundance toward the tail

**Diet:** Aquatic vertebrates and invertebrates; also aquatic vegetation

**Breeding:** Spawning season August–December with peak activity in October. Usually occurs at night among submerged vegetation at temperatures of 68–77°F (20–25°C ). Eggs laid during a period of about 1 hour and then apparently abandoned. Hatching occurs 3 weeks later. Growth of larvae is slow, and it is not known at what age or size maturity is reached. Life span up to 50 years

**Related endangered species:** None

**Status:** Not listed by IUCN; CITES II

Queensland

AUSTRALIA

New South Wales

# Lynx, Iberian

## *Lynx pardinus*

*The Iberian lynx, once widespread in Spain and Portugal, may now be the world's most endangered cat. Although legally protected since the 1970s, it is still endangered as a result of habitat loss, persecution, and threats to its prey.*

The Iberian lynx is smaller than the European lynx, but otherwise similar. Although previously widespread in Spain and Portugal, it is now a rare species. By the 1980s there were probably fewer than 1,200 lynxes alive. By 1999 the population had halved, and the distribution of the lynx had contracted by more than 80 percent in fewer than 30 years. Today there are probably fewer than 600 lynxes left. The main population of about 400 animals lives in the mountains of central southern Spain. The rest are widely scattered, and all these subpopulations have a total of fewer than 100 animals.

The Iberian lynxes live in open woodland with scattered pines and evergreen oaks. They also favor thick scrub, patches of open grassland, and dense thickets of dry scrub on the mountains. Rabbits comprise 80 percent of their diet, a degree of specialization that is dangerous in a changing world. To rely too much on one source of food makes any animal vulnerable if something goes wrong with the supply. In the 1950s the viral disease myxomatosis swept through the rabbit populations of Europe, killing over 90 percent of them in some places. As the years went by, the rabbit population became more resistant to this fatal disease, and numbers began to recover. However, in the late 1980s a new disaster struck in the form of rabbit hemorrhagic disease, which also killed large numbers of rabbits, again leaving few to support the lynx population.

## Habitat Loss

The rapid economic development of Spain and Portugal over recent decades has been a significant threat to the lynx. Remote parts of the countryside have been opened up by the construction of new roads. Hotels and vacation homes have been built to accommodate the booming tourist industry and provide facilities for retirement communities. Overstocking of cattle and game ranches and the erection of deer fencing have also had a detrimental

FRANCE

SPAIN

PORTUGAL

ALGERIA

## DATA PANEL

**Iberian lynx (pardel lynx)**

*Lynx pardinus*

**Family:** Felidae

**World population:** 500–600

**Distribution:** Parts of Spain and Portugal

**Habitat:** Open pine woodland and among dense, dry thickets of scrub on the mountains

**Size:** Length head/body: 31.5 in–38 in (80–96 cm); tail: 3.5–4.5 in (9–11 cm); height at shoulder: 24–27 in (60–68 cm). Weight: 22–33 lb (10–15 kg)

**Form:** A large, long-legged cat, with a short black-tipped tail and tufted ears. Coat pale brown with white spots

**Diet:** Mainly rabbits, but also young deer, rodents, and ground-dwelling birds

**Breeding:** Breeding season January–March, births in May. Litters of 2–3 kittens born; 1 litter per year. Life span unknown, but other lynx species live up to 15 years

**Related endangered species:** Cheetah (*Acinonyx jubatus*)* VU; tiger (*Panthera tigris*)* EN; snow leopard (*Uncia uncia*)* EN; several other big and small cats

**Status:** IUCN EN; CITES I

**See also:** Organizations **1:** 10; Populations **1:** 20; Cat, Iriomote **3:** 30; Ocelot, Texas **7:** 20; Wildcat **10:** 62

**The Iberian lynx** *has an attractive gray-brown mottled coat, a broad, short head, and distinctive tufted ears. It is now one of the world's rarest mammals.*

effect on the habitat for many forms of wildlife, including the lynx. The natural mosaic of habitats that suits lynxes and their prey has been broken up, and the lynx population has been reduced and critically fragmented into nine separate subpopulations, with a total of at least 48 separate breeding groups. Increased use of roads has meant more deaths, particularly in the Coto Doñana area, and some populations of lynx already have fewer than 10 females, so even a few road kills per year could be disastrous.

## Persecution

Although lynxes have been legally protected in Spain since 1973 and Portugal since 1974, many are still shot. Most live on private estates and cattle ranches, where hunting and shooting are common. Only 40 to 50 lynxes live in the protected area of the Coto Doñana National Park; very few enjoy the protection of nature reserves. Lynxes have now been infected with tuberculosis (TB) from wild pigs and deer.

## Action Plan

An action plan for the lynx now exists: The European Habitats Directive has given the species more protection, and there should be money available from the European Union to manage the countryside in a manner more suited to wildlife conservation. However, it may all have come too late to save the Iberian lynx.

# Macaque, Barbary

*Macaca sylvanus*

*The Barbary macaques that live on the Rock of Gibraltar are well looked after and protected. The same cannot be said for the species in North Africa, where numbers have declined dramatically in recent years.*

Because the Barbary macaque's tail is virtually nonexistent, the species is sometimes known as the Barbary ape; apes are often defined as "monkeys without tails." The Barbary macaque is, in fact, a monkey. It is the only member of the macaque subfamily to live in Africa—all its close relatives come from Asia. In addition, it is the only primate to live in the wild in Europe, although whether or not its presence there is natural is the subject of much scientific debate.

A very small population of Barbary macaques lives on the British-owned Rock of Gibraltar. Some scientists are convinced that this population is descended from macaques that, according to fossil evidence, once lived all over Europe. Others insist that the Gibraltar macaques were brought to Europe from North Africa long after their ancestors had become extinct. What is certain is that the Gibraltar population has been boosted by deliberate introductions from Africa, most famously during World War II, when the Gibraltar population declined to just seven animals. An old superstition warned that if Gibraltar ever lost the macaques, then Britain would lose the Rock. As a morale-boosting exercise the British prime minister, Winston Churchill, arranged for more monkeys to be transported from Africa.

## Resourceful Creatures

Whatever their true origins, the Barbary macaques of Gibraltar are secure and at risk of little more than catching human diseases from tourists. There are about 100 of them, and they are well fed and protected; there is even an army officer appointed to cater to their needs.

Life for the vast majority of Barbary macaques is not so luxurious, however. In the rest of their range they live in pine and oak forests on the slopes of the Atlas Mountains in North Africa. Winters are harsh, and the monkeys need their extrathick coats to survive the cold.

Like all monkeys, Barbary macaques are resourceful when it comes to finding food. They will readily supplement their natural diet of leaves, fruit, and acorns by raiding crops from fields or plantations and

## DATA PANEL

**Barbary macaque (Barbary ape)**

***Macaca sylvanus***

**Family:** Cercopithecidae

**World population:** About 15,000

**Distribution:** Morocco, Tunisia, and Gibraltar

**Habitat:** Montane (mountainous) woodland and rocky mountain slopes

**Size:** Length: 24 in (60 cm); height at shoulder: 18–20 in (45–50 cm). Weight: 10–20 lb (4.5–9 kg)

**Form:** Grayish-brown monkey with no obvious tail; face hairless with longish nose and capacious cheek pouches; arms and legs about the same length

**Diet:** Fruit, leaves, seeds, shoots, acorns, tubers, insects (especially caterpillars), bark, and pine needles

**Breeding:** Single young born at any time of year after 7-month gestation. New sibling arrives 1 year later; males help care for young; maturity at 4 years

**Related endangered species:** Mentawai macaque (*Macaca pagensis*) CR; lion-tailed macaque (*M. silenus*) EN; Japanese macaque (*M. fuscata*)* DD

**Status:** IUCN VU; CITES II

thieving other human food from storage. The macaques are also exceedingly curious and will steal all kinds of inedible objects; stealing increases as human settlement and cultivated land spread farther up into the mountains, eroding the monkey's habitat.

## Losing Out

Not surprisingly, the macaques are unpopular, and they end up losing first their homes and then their lives to the farmers. The numbers and range of the macaques have diminished sharply. Barbary macaques were once found widely across North Africa, but now they are reduced to a few scattered populations. They have not been singled out for any special protection, although all primates are automatically listed on CITES Appendix II.

Several factors count against the macaques. Because they breed slowly—a mother Barbary macaque devotes an entire year to raising a single youngster—populations are slow to recover from losses. Macaques live in large troops with a strict social hierarchy, so simply releasing captive-bred individuals into the wild is unlikely to succeed. The best option for conserving the Barbary macaques is to preserve their habitat, but the area in which they live is poor; the growing human population needs land for cultivating crops, so conservation is low on their list of priorities.

**Barbary macaques** *have arms and legs of about the same length, well-suited to their life both in trees and on the ground. They are omnivorous monkeys, with large cheek pouches in which to store food.*

# Macaque, Japanese

## *Macaca fuscata*

*The Japanese macaque uses a combination of adaptability and intelligence to survive climatic conditions that would defeat other monkeys. However, these adaptations are no match for decades of habitat destruction and persecution by humans.*

The Japanese macaque lives farther north than any other nonhuman primate. Its range extends well into the temperate zone, so it has to contend with the varied challenges of the changing seasons. The Japanese macaques that live farthest north on the large island of Honshu regularly have to deal with winter temperatures as low as –59° F (–15° C). Just like humans, macaques in certain areas have realized that there is nothing quite like a hot bath for beating the cold, and entire troops spend long periods wallowing in thermal pools that are fed by hot springs.

The harsh winters in northern Japan can make food difficult to find. During the warmer months the macaques eat well, feeding on seasonal fruits, flowers, leaves, and seeds; in winter they are reduced to stripping bark and nibbling off newly formed flower buds to survive. One scientific study estimated that most northern Japanese macaques got less than half the protein and just over half the calories they needed during the winter. The monkeys must therefore live off their fat reserves for many weeks until spring brings more food.

## Persecution by Humans

Life is a little less harsh for the macaques living farther south, but throughout their range Japanese macaques are also facing serious challenges of another kind. Macaques are susceptible to many human diseases and are often used in medical research. Today most research animals are bred in captivity, but for many years Japanese macaques were taken from the wild and transported to laboratories all over the world. Since many macaques died in transit, far more were taken than were actually needed. This appalling practice accounted for the lives of thousands of macaques every year.

Despite the fact that macaques are now protected by Japanese law, many still die at the hands of humans. Large areas of their forest habitat have already been cleared, mostly to make space for crops to feed Japan's human population. As the macaques' habitat shrinks, the remaining animals use their initiative to find alternative sources of food. Often, they turn to the newly created orchards, orange groves, and crop fields that stand where their original food

---

## DATA PANEL

**Japanese macaque**

*Macaca fuscata*

**Family:** Cercopithecidae

**World population:** 35,000–50,000 (1990 estimate)

**Distribution:** Japan

**Habitat:** Montane forest (forest found in mountainous areas)

**Size:** Length: 24–48 in (60–120 cm). Weight: 22–66 lb (10–30 kg)

**Form:** Distinctive red-faced monkey, with thick gray or light-brown fur on rest of body; short tail

**Diet:** Mostly fruit; some seeds, leaves, flowers, bark, and insects

**Breeding:** Single young born April–September after gestation of 5–6 months; mature at 3 years. Lives up to 20 years in captivity, fewer in the wild

**Related endangered species:** Mentawai macaque *(Macaca pagensis)* CR; lion-tailed macaque *(M. silenus)* EN; Barbary macaque *(M. sylvanus)** VU

**Status:** IUCN DD; CITES I

---

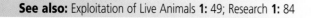

**The Japanese macaque** *is well adapted to the harsh winters of northern Japan. It has a thick coat and—unlike macaques in warmer parts of the world—a short tail. One theory is that a short tail is less prone to frostbite than a longer one.*

## Intelligent Creatures

Extensive studies on troops of Japanese macaques have revealed all kinds of fascinating behavior. One particular individual, a female the researchers called Imo, started washing her food to make it taste better. Usually monkeys just brush dirt and sand off their food, but Imo washed sweet potatoes in a nearby stream. Before long, the whole troop had picked up the habit.

Another innovation credited to Imo was sorting grain from sand by tossing handfuls into the stream. The sand would sink, while the floating grain could be scooped back off the surface. While these activities clearly demonstrated the use of intelligence in practical matters, macaques have also been found to use their skills in playful behavior. For example, several troops of macaques were reported making snowballs, starting with a small, hand-molded ball, then making it bigger by rolling it through the snow. These endearing characteristics have won the Japanese macaque many friends, and it is to be hoped that the animals will soon be granted the space and freedom from persecution that they badly need.

source used to be. Farmers regard the macaques as pests, and many flaunt the law by shooting the animals to protect their crops. In addition, human settlement has spread so close to the macaques' habitat that the monkeys have also become a nuisance in urban areas: It is not uncommon for them to wander into towns in search of food.

# Macaw, Hyacinth

### *Anodorhynchus hyacinthinus*

*The world's largest parrot, the hyacinth macaw is a spectacular vivid blue South American bird. It has suffered a massive decline in numbers over the last 40 years due mainly to illegal trapping for private collectors.*

Once relatively numerous across much of its range in Brazil, the hyacinth macaw is now rare in most of its former strongholds. The largest population occurs in the Brazilian part of the Pantanal region—a huge, grassy plain about the size of Iowa that straddles the southwestern Brazilian states of Mato Grosso and Mato Grosso do Sul, extending southeast into Bolivia and Paraguay. Dotted with palms and other trees and shrubs, the habitat is flooded during the rainy season, peaking in about February to become the biggest freshwater wetland in the world. Even here numbers of the great blue parrots have declined alarmingly in recent times.

The two other, smaller, populations are in the Gerais region of central Brazil and in Amazonia.

In contrast to most of the more familiar macaws of the genus *Ara*, such as the blue-and-yellow and scarlet macaws, which eat a wide range of plants, hyacinth macaws depend on a few species of palm trees for their staple diet of palm nuts.

The massive black bill of the hyacinth macaw is an adaptation to its specialized diet. Accounting for about one-fifth of the entire weight of the bird and worked by powerful muscles, it is immensely strong and forms an impressive and efficient tool for crushing the large, hard nuts of palm trees.

As well as taking them straight from the trees, the birds also feed on the palm nuts where they have fallen on the ground. On ranchlands where cattle are raised they can take advantage of concentrations of palm nuts that remain undigested in cowpats. The cattle digest the soft, fleshy mesocarp surrounding each nut, thereby saving the birds the effort.

Although birds in northeastern Brazil nest on remote cliff crevices, most hyacinth macaws need suitable nesting trees if they are to breed. In the Pantanal only a few of the trees grow big enough to have developed large hollows in which the birds can conceal their nests from predators. However, such big trees and big birds are so prominent that local people cannot fail to be aware of the nest sites. Sometimes, trappers return year after year to steal chicks, while other long-established nesting trees are felled or burned by landowners clearing the land for cattle; both scenarios spell disaster for the hyacinth macaws.

Habitat in the Gerais region is being rapidly converted to mechanized agriculture, cattle ranches, and exotic tree plantations.

## Illegal Trade

During the period between 1970 and 1980 huge numbers of young hyacinth macaws were taken from their nests and sold to dealers or middlemen, who then sold them on to private collectors in the United States, Europe, Japan, and other countries. Some illegal trade still exists. An equal but persistent demand for captive macaws within Brazil, and the taking of birds for feather headdresses or food adds to the problem, despite Brazilian legislation protecting the species. Estimates suggest that up to 10,000 hyacinth macaws may have been taken from the wild in the 1980s alone.

In 1987 the situation regarding international trade was judged to be so serious that the hyacinth macaw was moved from Appendix II to Appendix I of CITES, but for a while this had the unfortunate effect of

### DATA PANEL

**Hyacinth macaw (hyacinthine macaw, blue macaw, black macaw)**

*Anodorhynchus hyacinthinus*

**Family:** Psittacidae

**World population:** About 2,500–10,000 individuals in Brazil; perhaps fewer than 100 in Bolivia; small numbers in Paraguay

**Distribution:** Three main areas of interior Brazil: on the southern side of the Amazon in the northeast; the Gerais region of central Brazil; the seasonally flooded Pantanal region of the Upper Río Paraguay basin, just extending into eastern Bolivia and northern Paraguay

**Habitat:** Lightly wooded areas, especially where clumps of trees are mixed with open grassland or swamps

**Size:** Length: 35–39 in (90–100 cm)

**Form:** Bird of great size with huge, hooked black bill; long, narrow wings; long tail; cobalt-blue plumage, purple on wings and tail, blackish on underwings and undertail

**Diet:** Mainly nuts of various palm trees; fruit, including figs; occasionally water snails; liquid from unripe palm fruits

**Breeding:** Usually in dry season; 2 (rarely 1 or 3) eggs laid; incubation 3–4 weeks, fledging about 3.5 months

**Related endangered species:** Lear's macaw (*Anodorhynchus leari*) CR; glaucous macaw (*A. glaucus*) CR; Spix's macaw (*Cyanopsitta spixii*)* CR; blue-throated macaw (*Ara glaucogularis*) EN; military macaw (*A. militaris*) VU; red-fronted macaw (*A. rubrogenys*) EN; blue-winged macaw (*Propyrrhura maracana*) VU

**Status:** IUCN EN; CITES I

stimulating even greater demand by unscrupulous dealers and collectors willing to pay $8,000 or more for each bird.

Recent efforts to save the hyacinth macaw have included studies of its ecology, an investigation into trade in the bird, and the establishment of nest boxes. Most encouragingly, many ranch owners in the Pantanal and Gerais regions no longer allow trapping on their properties.

**The hyacinth macaw** *is a slow breeder, taking about five months from egg-laying to fledging (the time when the young start to fly). The birds rarely succeed in rearing more than one of the usual two chicks.*

# Macaw, Spix's

### *Cyanopsitta spixii*

*Since the discovery of a single survivor in 1990 this beautiful Brazilian parrot has been the world's rarest bird. Tragically, the only surviving wild bird has now disappeared.*

The scientific world became aware of Spix's macaw in 1820, when the German zoologist and Munich museum director Johann Wagler described a specimen that had been shot for the museum by his colleague Johann Spix, in whose honor he named the bird. For the following 150 years the beautiful blue parrot was known only from a handful of museum specimens and birds collected for the cage-bird trade. The species was probably always scarce; and although it may have ranged over a much wider area of northeastern Brazil, records from many areas were misidentifications.

## Rediscovery and Decline

In the 1980s three to five Spix's macaws were found living in woodland near the São Francisco River in Bahia state in the interior of northeastern Brazil. The humid gallery woodland forms an oasis in the otherwise dry scrubland known as caatinga that dominates this part of Brazil. It contains both the tall caraiba trees the birds need for nesting and the trees that provide it with its seed and fruit diet.

By the late 1980s only three small fragments of caraiba woodland remained in Bahia. The macaws' special habitat had all but vanished as a result of chronic grazing pressure from the cattle introduced by ranchers from the late 18th century and settlers clearing the land for crops. With their habitat reduced, the macaws were more vulnerable not only to trapping by local people to supply cage-bird enthusiasts, but also to hunting for food. They may also have suffered from invasions of hybrid bees (locally known as "killer bees") that were reported to occupy nest sites and kill incubating parrots in the area. Since the few remaining wild birds were close relatives, they were vulnerable to the consequences of inbreeding.

Tragically, in 1987 and 1988 the three known remaining birds were caught by trappers for the cage-bird trade, and there were no further sightings. In 1989 Spix's macaw was declared Extinct in the Wild.

BRAZIL

BOLIVIA

PARAGUAY

## DATA PANEL

**Spix's macaw (little blue macaw)**

*Cyanopsitta spixii*

**Family:** Psittacidae

**World population:** Last wild male is probably dead; 66 in captivity

**Distribution:** Restricted to a very small area in the state of Bahia, northeastern Brazil

**Habitat:** For breeding seems to need gallery woodland dominated by caraiba trees; also needs trees of spurge family to supply food

**Size:** Length: 21.5–22.5 in (55–57 cm)

**Form:** Slender, medium-sized macaw with square-shaped head and long tail and wings; blue and blue-gray plumage; head grayish blue; upperparts brighter blue with violet tinge on back; black bill

**Diet:** Seeds and fruit of trees, chiefly 4 members of spurge family

**Breeding:** Breeding season usually November–March; nests in tree hollow in which the female lays 2–3 white eggs

**Related endangered species:** Hyacinth macaw (*Anodorhynchus hyacinthinus*)* EN; Lear's macaw (*A. leari*) CR; glaucous macaw (*A. glaucus*) CR are closest relatives; 5 other species of macaw are threatened, including the blue-throated macaw (*Ara glaucogularis*) CR and blue-winged macaw (*Propyrrhura maracana*) VU

**Status:** IUCN CR; CITES I and II

**See also:** Exploitation of Live Animals **1:** 49; Genetics **1:** 56; Amazon, St. Vincent **2:** 14; Macaw, Hyacinth **6:** 58

**Spix's macaw** *is the smallest of the four species of blue macaw, all of which occur— or occurred—in Brazil.*

However, in 1990 a lone male was found at the same site. This prompted the Permanent Committee for the Recovery of Spix's Macaw to establish a base camp at the site to study the bird.

In 1995 an attempt was made to reintroduce a captive-bred female in the hope that she would mate with the wild male. This plan became celebrated in Brazil, and a children's book helped raise the profile of the bird.

Sadly, the program was a disaster. Although the two birds paired after about two months, the female vanished less than a month later and is thought to have been killed after collision with a power line. The wild male returned to a female blue-winged macaw with whom he had paired earlier. This is a Vulnerable species that, although not a very close relative, lived alongside Spix's macaws.

Blue-winged macaw eggs were introduced to the odd couple's nest to see if they could hatch them and raise the chicks, but the eggs were taken by predators. The Recovery Committee decided to introduce young blue-winged macaw chicks to the nest, and the foster parents successfully raised them to the fledging stage. The scene was now set for a plan to transfer chicks from a captive pair in Brazil.

## Without Trace

Tragically, despite having been guarded, the single wild male disappeared in 2000. The bird's age was estimated at about 19 years, and he may have died of a disease or been killed by a predator. Such a fate is more likely than capture for the cage-bird trade, because of the powerful support among the local people for Spix's macaw.

The survival of the lone male had been of great importance in trying to reintroduce captive-bred birds to the wild. Spix's macaw had a restricted diet; the last wild survivor used to fly over 37 miles (60 km) in search of food in the dry season, and he would have built up detailed knowledge of his surroundings and the best times and places to find food. He could have passed on such knowledge to the released captive birds. For this reason any future reintroduction plans will be carefully considered.

# Magpie-Robin, Seychelles

## Copsychus sechellarum

*The Seychelles magpie-robin's tiny population was rescued from extinction by a conservation program. Although numbers are increasing, it remains in a critical situation.*

The Seychelles magpie-robin has black-and-white plumage characteristic of some magpies, but it is not a magpie. Although it lacks the red breast of the famous American robin, it is a member of the thrush family to which the robin also belongs. Unlike the robin, it is an extremely rare bird. An ambitious conservation program is now starting to show real success in bringing it back from the brink of extinction.

The decline of the Seychelles magpie-robin follows a pattern all too familiar among the fauna of remote islands. It was once fairly widespread on at least six of the granitic islands of the group, which are situated some 620 miles (1,000 km) northeast of the other small coral islands and atolls of the Seychelles archipelago in the Indian Ocean. Its former range was small—the total land area of the 20 granitic Seychelles islands is only about 93 square miles (240 sq. km).

### A Variety of Threats

Once settlers and their domestic animals took up residence on the islands, there was little scope for retreat. The magpie-robin was capable of adapting to the almost total loss of native vegetation that followed in the wake of forest clearance and increased cultivation. However, this tame, ground-feeding bird was unable to withstand the combined threats of introduced rats and domestic cats. The rats ate the birds' eggs and young, while the cats took recently fledged immatures and adults.

By 1965 the combined assault by the two alien mammals had completely removed the magpie-robin from all but one rat-free island, Frégate, and there the species was in decline. Predation by feral cats may have been responsible for the decline, but the population failed to recover after they were eradicated. The world population stood at a precarious 12 to 15 individuals.

Clearly other factors were involved. Three other introduced predators—the common myna, barn owl, and brown rat (which invaded Frégate from an unknown source in 1995)—competed with the magpie-robins for a limited food supply. Shortages around nest sites meant that the young were likely to starve.

## DATA PANEL

**Seychelles magpie-robin**

*Copsychus sechellarum*

**Family:** Turdidae

**World population:** 85 birds

**Distribution:** Originally inhabited at least 6 of the granitic islands of the Seychelles, but by 1965 survived only on Frégate; introduced to Cousin, Cousine, and Aride

**Habitat:** Originally mature native coastal forest; today in remnant mature central woodland, plantations, and vegetable gardens

**Size:** Length: 7–8.3 in (18–21 cm)

**Form:** Thrushlike; tail often held cocked; plumage glossy black with a dark blue sheen; has a white bar on the upper half of each wing; feet and legs black; juveniles have duller plumage, lacking the gloss, and gray-brown edges to their white wing bars

**Diet:** Mainly a wide range of invertebrates, including termites, scorpions, and giant millipedes; also small vertebrates, such as lizards (skinks and geckos), fish, other birds' eggs, and fruit

**Breeding:** Breeds all year round; the nest is an untidy jumble of vegetation with a neat cup in the middle and is sited in a hole in a large tree (now also in nest boxes) or in the crown of a large coconut palm; lays a single pale-blue egg

**Related endangered species:** The only one in the same genus is the black shama (*Copsychus cebuensis*) EN

**Status:** IUCN CR; not listed by CITES

KENYA

Islands of Frégate, Cousin, Cousine, and Aride

SEYCHELLES

TANZANIA

COMOROS

MOZAMBIQUE

MADAGASCAR

MAURITIUS

Réunion (France)

**See also:** Introductions 1: 54; Disease 1: 55; Asity, Yellow-Bellied 2: 32

**The Seychelles magpie-robin** *is an engagingly tame bird, a trait that once made it an easy target for hunters and introduced predators.*

Deterioration of the habitat was another problem facing the birds. The species' requirements are a combination of tall trees (to provide nest sites, perches, and shade) and open ground with bare soil and leaf litter in which to forage for a variety of mainly invertebrate prey. Originally, the magpie-robins were birds of mature, native coastal forest, but the forest was felled by early settlers—initially for timber and to grow spices, then for coconut plantations and for firewood to fuel the cinnamon distilleries. Fortunately, the magpie-robins adapted to living in the mature woodland that remains on the central plateaus, as well as in vegetable gardens and plantations.

In recent times, however, dense plant cover has spread over abandoned plantation areas, making the habitat unsuitable for the birds. In addition, the magpie-robins have been threatened by pesticides used to control insects in hotels and houses. Attempts to poison the brown rats on Frégate had to be abandoned when three magpie-robins died after eating affected invertebrates.

## Recovery Program

In 1990 BirdLife International—a global partnership of conservation organizations—working with the government of the Seychelles and the owner of Frégate, set up a recovery program for the magpie-robin. Birds were moved from the island to small, predator-free islands. Breeding success was improved by the provision of nest boxes, protection from predators, creation of suitable habitat, supplementary feeding, and control of common myna numbers. By 1994 the population on Frégate had increased to 48 birds, with two birds translocated to the island of Aride. In 1999, after further translocations of birds, the total population reached an all-time high of 85 individuals: 46 on Frégate, 23 on Cousin, 15 on Cousine, and one on Aride. Conservationists are now carrying out a pest-management program. Research on the factors affecting the quality of the birds' habitat is underway, as is a study of the birds' genetic makeup, in an attempt to investigate inbreeding.

The introduction of the magpie-robin to Aride has faced an additional problem: The birds have been infected by a pathogenic bacteria, and it is a priority of the conservation team to investigate this. Other targets include the eradication of brown rats from Frégate without harming the magpie-robins and selecting three other islands to move the birds to when introduced mammals have been removed and suitable habitat restored. It is hoped that by 2006 there will be more than 200 magpie-robins on seven islands, enabling the species to be downgraded from Critically Endangered to Endangered.

# Malleefowl

*Leipoa ocellata*

*Instead of using body heat to hatch its eggs—like almost all other birds—the remarkable malleefowl constructs a giant mound of rotting vegetation that generates enough heat to act as an incubator. Once widespread, the species is now threatened by a variety of factors.*

The malleefowl's nest mound—at up to 16 feet (5 m) wide and 5 feet (1.5 m) high—is one of the largest structures made by any bird. It is built mainly by the male, one of the most industrious of all bird fathers. Preparing the mound may take him as long as four months, and he tends it for much of the rest of the year. He begins work in the Australian fall (April or May), using his powerful, sturdy feet to dig out a large crater, or foundation. He then rakes in masses of leaves, twigs, and bark gathered from the surrounding area. Finally, after allowing the winter rains to thoroughly soak the mound, he covers it with a layer of soil or sand. Sealed inside the layer, the dampened vegetation rots, and the process of fermentation produces heat.

Starting in the spring (about September) and extending over a period of about seven months, the female lays her eggs. She deposits one at a time every four to 17 days into a small chamber in the top of the pile. Throughout the laying period the male visits the mound regularly to ensure that the temperature in the egg chamber stays at a more or less constant average of 91°F (33°C). He often sticks his bill into the mound; researchers believe that the birds use receptors on their tongue or in their mouth to check the temperature precisely. The male will open the mound to let the heat produced by the rotting vegetation escape or, later—when fermentation is nearly over—to allow the sun to warm the mound. He also adds or removes the layer of soil, just like someone adjusting the number of blankets on a bed.

After an unusually long incubation period for a bird of the malleefowl's size (generally lasting about nine weeks) each

AUSTRALIA

## DATA PANEL

**Malleefowl**

*Leipoa ocellata*

**Family:** Megapodiidae

**World population:** Fewer than 100,000 pairs

**Distribution:** Parts of southwestern and southern Australia

**Habitat:** Semidesert mallee (scrub); also mulga (acacia) scrub and dry coastal heaths

**Size:** Length: about 24 in (60 cm). Weight: males 4.5 lb (2.1 kg); females 3.3–4.4 lb (1.5–2 kg)

**Form:** Large chickenlike bird; pale grayish plumage barred with black, gray, dull chestnut, buff, and white; male has flattened crest

**Diet:** Mainly seeds, fruit, buds, and flowers; also cockroaches, ants, dragonflies, beetles, spiders, bees, and fungi

**Breeding:** Male starts mound in April or May; female usually lays 15–24 pale pink eggs from mid-September to October; incubation usually takes about 9 weeks

**Related endangered species:** Niuafoou scrubfowl (*Megapodius pritchardii*) CR; Micronesian scrubfowl (*M. laperouse*) EN; Bruijn's brush-turkey (*Aepypodius bruijnii*) VU; maleo (*Macrocephalon maleo*) VU; Nicobar scrubfowl (*Megapodius nicobariensis*) VU; Vanuatu scrubfowl (*M. layardi*) VU; Moluccan scrubfowl (*M. wallacei*) VU

**Status:** IUCN VU; not listed by CITES

**See also:** Introductions **1:** 54; Guan, Horned **5:** 44; Peafowl, Congo **7:** 60; Tragopan, Temminck's **9:** 94

chick hatches at a very advanced stage of development. It immediately forces its way through about 20 inches (50 cm) of mound material to the surface and, after a brief rest from its efforts, is able to fly away and feed itself on its first day. Neither parent plays any part in the rearing of their young.

## Challenging Times

Malleefowl are primarily birds of arid, mallee scrub dominated by dwarf eucalyptus trees. Many such areas, especially in the southwest, are also suitable for wheat, and a major reason for the huge decline of the species over the last 50 years is the relentless expansion of agriculture. It is not only crops that damage the malleefowl's habitat. Cattle, sheep, and introduced weeds wipe out wild plants, while fires and land clearance also take their toll.

Alien predators, especially the red fox (introduced by Europeans in the 1850s for hunting), kill many malleefowl. The chicks' habit of "freezing" when danger threatens protects them from hawks and other native predators but makes them easy game for foxes.

Conservation programs are attempting to reverse the fortunes of the malleefowl. Initiatives include enlisting the help of landowners and conservation groups to monitor the birds, education programs, captive breeding, and extensive fox culling, as well as the replanting of native vegetation and establishment of "corridors" to link areas of suitable habitat.

**The malleefowl** *is named after its habitat of mallee—scrubland that occupies much of semiarid southern Australia.*

# Manakin, Black-Capped

*Piprites pileatus*

*This attractive little bird is classed as Vulnerable because its population is known to be small and is probably declining as a result of the large-scale destruction and fragmentation of the southeastern part of Brazil's montane Atlantic forest, the only place in which it is known to live today.*

This is a rare and sparsely distributed species, restricted to the forested mountains inland from the Atlantic coast of southeastern Brazil. Even within this area the manakin only occurs in a limited number of places, including the Itatiaia massif in the state of Minas Gerais and specific sites in the states of Rio de Janeiro, São Paulo, Paraná, Santa Catarina, and Rio Grande do Sul. The only other place where the species has been seen is in the extreme northeast of Argentina, where a single individual was collected in 1959 in the department of Misiones.

In these sites the birds are usually seen in regions of humid, montane, Atlantic forest dominated by two types of conifer: a podocarp species, *Podocarpus lamberti*, and the Paraná pine, an araucaria species that is closely related to the monkey-puzzle trees of Argentina and Chile. They have also been observed in the understory of a dense bamboo thicket.

The birds have usually been seen singly, although sometimes also as part of mixed-species flocks, foraging in the dense forest canopy and subcanopy. The manakin feeds on a mixed diet of insects and other invertebrates that it picks off leaves, either when perched on a branch or twig or while hovering in the air. It also consumes the fruit of various trees, including *Geonoma* palms, *Rapanea*, and *Leandra*.

## Uncertain Relationships

The black-capped manakin has only two close relatives: the wing-barred manakin of much of northern South America and the gray-headed manakin of parts of Central America. All three have distinctive plumage and are quite easy to identify, and all live in the canopy and edges of humid tropical forests. The genus to which they belong, *Piprites*, is taxonomically controversial. Although it has long been classified in the manakin family, ornithologists have recently drawn attention to a number of anatomical differences separating its three species from the typical manakins. One well-known expert on Brazilian birds has gone further, suggesting that the *Piprites* species should be grouped with the cotingas.

## DATA PANEL

**Black-capped manakin**

*Piprites pileatus*

**Family:** Pipridae

**World population:** Estimated at 2,500–10,000 birds

**Distribution:** Very sparsely distributed in southeastern Brazil, from the state of Rio de Janeiro south to the northern part of the state of Rio Grande do Sul; also 1 confirmed record from extreme northeastern Argentina

**Habitat:** Montane Atlantic forest from 3,000–6,600 ft (900–2,000 m), mainly in areas dominated by Paraná pine (*Araucaria angustifolia*) and *Podocarpus lamberti* trees

**Size:** Length: 5 in (12 cm)

**Form:** Small, large-headed bird with short, thick, yellow bill, orange-yellow legs and feet, and reddish-brown and black plumage; has black cap and nape, rich chestnut back, rump, and wing-coverts; wings mainly black with yellow fringes and yellow patch at base of primary flight feathers; tail mainly chestnut but with black central feathers; face and underparts buff grading into pale yellow. Female somewhat duller, with olive back and indistinct pale-grayish wing-bars

**Diet:** Insects and other invertebrates; also fruit

**Breeding:** Details not recorded; may breed in the Southern Hemisphere spring

**Related endangered species:** Araripe manakin (*Antilophia bokermanni*) CR; Wied's tyrant-manakin (*Neopelma aurifrons*) EN; golden-crowned manakin (*Pipra vilasboasi*) VU; yellow-headed manakin (*Chloropipo flavicapilla*) LRnt

**Status:** IUCN VU; not listed by CITES

BOLIVIA
BRAZIL
PARAGUAY
ARGENTINA
URUGUAY

**See also:** Habitat Loss 1: 38; National Parks 1: 92; Tanager, Seven-Colored 9: 54

To confuse matters further, the three *Piprites* species look and behave in the field like the becards, a subgroup within the great tyrant-flycatcher family. Because of their uncertain taxonomic status, some ornithologists now prefer to refer to the birds as "piprites" rather than "manakins," calling the Brazilian species, for instance, the black-capped piprites.

## Threats and Conservation

The araucaria-podocarpus forest where the manakin lives has suffered a great deal of destruction and degradation since Europeans first colonized Brazil. The coastal forest was the first part of South America to be settled, from 1500 onward. In the late 16th century the discovery of gold and diamonds prompted European settlers to move inland, and the montane forests also began to be cleared.

The mines were exhausted within a century, after which agriculture began to take over. In time huge areas of forest were cleared to make way for coffee, banana, and rubber plantations. In the state of Paraná alone an estimated 78 percent of the original araucaria-podocarpus forest had been cut down by 1965, and the destruction continues today.

Recent reports from Itatiaia National Park suggest that the manakin may migrate up and down the mountains at different times of year. If this finding proves correct, it would imply that the birds need continuous forest tracts through their entire altitudinal range, which stretches from 2,900 to 6,600 feet (900 to 2,000 m); otherwise the fragmentation of the forest risks disrupting the birds' migration pattern, to their detriment. On the brighter side, the black-capped manakin does not seem to be restricted solely to the araucaria-podocarpus forest, and the montane forests in the north of its range have fortunately suffered a good deal less destruction than those of the neighboring lowlands.

**The black-capped manakin** *is a rare bird now found only in mountain forests in southeastern Brazil.*

N.A

The species is already protected in Brazil and is known to occur in at least four wildlife reserves. To improve its chances of survival, conservationists are searching for fresh sites where the birds may be living. To help them find out whether the species is present, they play recordings of the bird's calls and listen for a response. If the species is found at many new sites, it may be taken off the IUCN's list of threatened animals. **67**

# Manatee, Florida

**_Trichechus manatus latirostris_**

_Coastal development and the impact of fast speedboats threaten the Florida manatee. However, provided that its simple needs can be accommodated, there is no reason why these charming animals should not remain reasonably numerous._

There are two subspecies of the Caribbean or West Indian manatee. One, the Florida manatee, occurs in rivers and along nearby coasts. The other—the Antillean manatee—lives farther south in similar habitats.

Manatees usually occur in small family groups. They are slow-moving, sluggish animals that normally live on the edge of the sea and in sheltered lagoons. They will not tolerate water cooler than about 68°F (20°C) and often gather in warm places such as the areas where power stations discharge warm water into the sea—Cape Canaveral, Fort Myers, and Apollo Beach in Tampa Bay, for example. In summer they disperse widely along coasts and rivers.

## Dangerous Waters

Manatees cannot come ashore since they have no hind limbs. When they breathe out, they become less buoyant and sink below the surface, where they paddle gently around seeking food. They can stay underwater for up to 30 minutes before they need to come up for air. For much of the time, however, they float around at the water surface looking like large logs, with only the tops of their backs visible. When floating, they are not easy to see, nor can they see far themselves.

In the coastal areas of Florida, where there are large numbers of water skiers, fast launches, and other boats, the waters have become unsafe for manatees. Many people have houses at the water's edge and use their boats for recreation, fishing, and transport. Collisions are frequent and often fatal for the manatees.

The number of boats and the disturbance caused by the huge increase in their use along the Florida coasts and lagoons have led to a steep decline in manatee numbers. It has been calculated that a reduction in manatee deaths of only 10 percent every year should be sufficient to allow the population to increase again. However, one obstacle to recovery is that manatees are very slow breeders, and even a small increase in adult mortality leads to a rapid decline in the population.

Apart from people (and some large sharks farther south than Florida), manatees have no natural predators. Nonetheless, for centuries people have killed them for their meat. Manatees are easy prey since they cannot swim fast or defend themselves effectively. Hunting is probably the main threat to manatees outside American waters; they also get tangled up and drown in commercial fishing nets.

Florida manatees are legally protected, and in certain places where the water is clear and they can be easily seen drifting around, they have become an important tourist attraction. Visitors and local people are paying more attention to this fascinating creature.

**See also:** Ecotourism 1: 90; Cow, Steller's Sea 3: 70; Dugong 4: 46

## Setting Limits

People using boats are asked to avoid shallow water near the edges of rivers and lagoons (where there is plenty of aquatic vegetation) favored by the manatees. By imposing speed limits on small craft and providing separate channels for boats, conservationists are working toward a more secure future for the Florida manatee. With such measures in place there is no reason why the manatee should not survive in reasonable numbers.

The United States Fish and Wildlife Service has recently created a special manatee sanctuary at Three Sisters Springs in the Crystal River. More than 250 manatees spend the winter there because it is pleasantly warm. Disturbances from launches and boats had been forcing the animals out into colder waters, but this area is now off limits to visitors and boats between November and March.

**The Florida manatee population** *suffered in 1996, when over 155 were found dead. Agricultural chemicals may have been the cause, although natural toxins from algae in the water could have been responsible.*

### DATA PANEL

**Florida manatee**

*Trichechus manatus latirostris*

**Family:** Trichechidae

**World population:** Florida subspecies 2,000–3,000; rest of the species probably 5,000–10,000

**Distribution:** Coast of the Gulf of Mexico north to Carolinas. Antillean subspecies extends around the Caribbean to southern Brazil

**Habitat:** Shallow, warm coastal waters; rivers and brackish water

**Size:** Length: 7–13 ft (2–4 m). Weight: up to 1,300 lb (590 kg); exceptionally up to 1.5 tons (1,500 kg)

**Form:** Large, sluggish animal; broad head and thick upper lip with spiky bristles; flippers at front but not at rear; tail flat, horizontal, and rounded

**Diet:** Wide assortment of floating and submerged water weeds, including water hyacinth and sea grass

**Breeding:** Single calf born May–September at intervals of 2–3 years after gestation of 11–13 months. Mature at 3–4 years. Life span up to 60 years

**Related endangered species:** Steller's sea cow (*Hydrodamalis gigas*)* EX; African manatee (*Trichechus senegalensis*) VU; Amazon manatee (*T. inunguis*) VU; dugong (*Dugong dugon*)* VU; Antillean manatee (*T. m. manatus*) VU

**Status:** IUCN VU; CITES I

# Mantella, Golden

## *Mantella aurantiaca*

*The golden mantella frog is only found in one small forest on the island of Madagascar. It is threatened by the destruction of its habitat and by the international pet trade in frogs.*

The golden mantella is one of a small group of frog species found only in Madagascar. It is brightly colored, poisonous, and active by day. It shares such characteristics with the poison-dart (dendrobatid) frogs of Central and South America. In evolutionary terms, however, the golden mantellas and poison-dart frogs are not related. The golden mantella thus represents an example of "convergent evolution" by which organisms come to closely resemble one another not as a result of common evolutionary ancestry, but through the action of natural selection (the survival of individuals best adjusted to their environment). The exact relationships of the mantellas are not clear. Some authorities put them in the large family Ranidae; others in a small family of their own: the Mantellidae.

Like the poison-dart frogs, the mantellas acquire poisonous compounds, called alkaloids, from their insect prey. They incorporate the toxic substances into secretions made in numerous poison glands in their skin. Predators that attack toxic, brightly colored prey quickly learn to associate the striking color pattern with an unpleasant experience and thereafter avoid that particular kind of prey.

### Terrestrial Mating

Unlike many frogs, mantellas do not mate in standing water. However, they need damp conditions to breed and consequently mate in the rainy season. Males call to females, producing a sound like a cricket's chirp that consists of a series of notes, with three "clicks" in each. When a receptive female approaches, the male clasps her in a brief amplexus (mating embrace), during which the eggs are laid in hollows in the damp soil. There are suggestions that fertilization is internal, but mating has not been properly observed. The eggs are whitish in color, and there are between 20 and 75 in a clutch. They hatch after about 14 days; the tadpoles push their way up to the soil surface and then wriggle over the damp ground to a nearby pool. There they complete their development, emerging as tiny frogs about two months later. In contrast to the vivid adult coloration, newly metamorphosed golden mantellas are green and black.

### A Race against Time

The golden mantella lives only in one small forest area between Beforona and Maramanga in western Madagascar. The forests of Madagascar have been largely destroyed. Trees have been felled over large areas to be exported as timber and to create land for agriculture. All kinds of animals that are unique to the island are threatened by such activity, and biologists are currently exploring the remaining forest fragments to catalog the endemic (native) fauna before it disappears. As a result of the intense exploration, a growing number of newly described Madagascan species, including mantellas, are emerging. A few years ago only three mantellas had been described, but the most recent analysis lists 12 species.

Mantellas are also threatened by international trade, being popular as pets in Europe, the United States, and elsewhere. Since they are small and mainly terrestrial, the frogs are relatively easy to keep in captivity. In addition, they can be induced to breed, a factor that may be crucial for their conservation. To date only the golden mantella is listed under CITES, but other mantella species may be added to the list.

**See also:** CITES **1:** 12; Habitat Loss **1:** 38; Frog, Red-Legged **5:** 10

## DATA PANEL

**Golden mantella**

*Mantella aurantiaca*

**Family:** Ranidae/Mantellidae

**World population:** Unknown

**Distribution:** Eastern Madagascar

**Habitat:** Deep leaf litter in wet tropical forests

**Size:** Length: 0.8–1.3 in (2–3 cm)

**Form:** Adults bright yellow, orange, or red; newly metamorphosed frogs green and black; black eyes

**Diet:** Small invertebrates

**Breeding:** Clutch of 20–75 whitish eggs laid in dark cavities on land; eggs hatch after about 14 days; tadpoles wriggle to small pools and emerge as tiny frogs about 2 months later

**Related endangered species:** Conservation status of other mantellas not yet evaluated by IUCN

**Status:** IUCN VU; CITES II

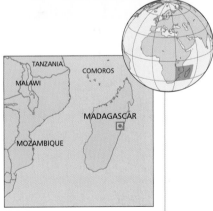

**Adult golden mantellas** *are both vividly colored and poisonous, a combination known as aposematic or warning coloration.*

**71**

# Markhor

*Capra falconeri*

*The impressive markhor, once common in the southern foothills of the Himalayas, has become rare in the wild as a direct result of centuries of hunting for its meat and its magnificent horns.*

The markhor is the world's largest goat and one of the most unusual-looking. Sadly, it is also one of the rarest. Just 50 years ago herds numbering well over 100 individuals were relatively common in the scrubby woodlands on the lower slopes of the western Himalayas. Today, however, the largest herds rarely exceed 30 markhors, with an average herd made up of just nine animals.

The herds move up and down the mountains with the seasons, reaching up to 13,000 feet (3,940 m) in midsummer but returning to 2,000 to 3,000 feet (610 to 910 m) to escape the worst of the winter weather. The largest herds consist of females and their offspring. Young markhors may stay with their mothers for up to two and a half years; their early lives are fraught with danger, with over 50 percent disappearing, presumed dead, in their first 18 months.

An adult male markhor in its winter breeding coat is a magnificent animal, with a shaggy mane around the neck and chest, and flowing "trousers" of long hair growing on the legs. The female has rather less flamboyant fringes of hair, but both sexes go back to a shorter, sleeker coat in summer.

## A Horny Problem

Undoubtedly the most remarkable features of the markhor are their splendid horns, which are present in both sexes. Unlike the antlers grown by male deer, the horns of goats and cattle are not cast off after the breeding season, but continue to grow throughout the animal's life. A huge pair of horns is therefore an unmistakable sign of a healthy and long-lived individual. The largest horns ever recorded were 5.3 feet (1.6 m) long, almost as long as the body of the goat that grew them. The horns of the female markhor rarely exceed 10 inches (25 cm) in length.

Despite being an obvious symbol of longevity and vigor, the male's horns are not just for show. They also make very effective weapons. Rival males lock horns and try to unbalance their opponent by shoving and twisting. Deadly earnest though the battles appear, such bouts tend to be tests of brute strength rather than genuine fights to the death, and a vanquished male will usually live to fight another day.

Sadly, however, the very horns that might make a particular male successful at winning mates may well be his undoing. Although strictly illegal, the trade in markhor horns is highly lucrative. Powdered horn is used in many traditional medicines, and a set of mounted horns makes a valuable hunting trophy. In China markhor horn changes hands at over $2,000 per pound. It is not surprising that some impoverished local people view the markhor as simply a larger and potentially more valuable version of their own domestic goats and are willing to supply the black market.

## Habitat Competition

Markhors also have their fair share of nonhuman predators, including wolves, snow leopards, and lynxes. In addition, steady encroachment of human settlement on the markhor's range and competition from domestic livestock for the limited grazing available make life difficult.

Of the three distinct subspecies of markhor, all are Endangered, and one, the Turkmenian markhor, is Critically Endangered. Even without the threat of habitat loss and illegal hunting, life is tough for the

**See also:** Specialization 1: 28; Luxury Products 1: 46; Ibex, Nubian 5: 70

## DATA PANEL

**Markhor**

*Capra falconeri*

**Family:** Bovidae

**World population:** Probably fewer than 6,000

**Distribution:** Himalayan regions of Afghanistan, Pakistan, India, Tajikistan, Uzbekistan, and Turkmenistan

**Habitat:** Scrubby woodland on mountain slopes

**Size:** Length: up to 6.2 ft (1.9 m); height to shoulder: up to 3.7 ft (1.2 m); females smaller than males. Weight: up to 242 lb (110 kg)

**Form:** Large shaggy-coated, pale-brown goat with distinctive corkscrewlike horns

**Diet:** Grass, leaves, twigs, and mast (nuts, including acorns)

**Breeding**: Between 1 and 3 kids born April–June. Life span at least 15 years

**Related endangered species:** Nubian ibex *(Capra nubiana)*\* EN; walia ibex *(C. walia)* CR; various other wild goats

**Status:** IUCN EN; CITES I

markhors. The animal's diet is relatively poor in nutrients, especially in winter, when they switch from grazing tussocky grasses to browsing twigs and leaves. In order to eat enough to survive, a typical markhor will spend between eight and 12 hours a day feeding, pausing briefly at midday to rest and chew the cud. Such a regime ensures the most effective possible digestion of its tough food.

**The name markhor,** *translated literally from the Persian, means snake-eater. The goats are vegetarian, but they will kill snakes in self-defense, and it is presumably from this that the name comes.*

# Marten, Pine

*Martes martes*

*In the 19th century culling by gamekeepers eliminated the pine marten from many parts of its range. Today the animal is more widely tolerated, and numbers are rising.*

The pine marten is a cat-sized member of the weasel family. Its shape and size vary considerably across its range. The largest specimens are found in Denmark and western Europe; smaller ones occur farther east.

Pine martens are mainly active at night and like to use hollow trees or cavities among rocks as dens in which to sleep, shelter, and raise their young. They are forest-dwelling animals that are well adapted to climbing and leaping among the trees, and are commonly found in conifer forests up to the treeline. However, they also like to feed in open grassy areas, where they hunt for voles and ground-nesting birds. In parts of Ireland and in Switzerland pine martens also feed extensively on ripe fruit in the fall.

There is a popular belief that pine martens prey on squirrels. Although they do occasionally take juveniles, they are not as agile in the branches as adult squirrels and therefore usually leave them alone. From time to time pine martens raid the nests of wild bees for honey or eat rabbits and lemmings—particularly if they are in plentiful supply.

## Easily Trapped

The pine marten is a very flexible, adaptable, and successful animal, yet it has become extinct in many areas, particularly southern Britain. Pine martens were widespread there even as late as the 19th century. However, the increasing popularity of shooting gamebirds on estates led to large numbers of gamekeepers being employed. It was their job to exterminate all predators that might kill the gamebirds, and the pine marten was especially victimized, being easily trapped or attracted to poisoned baits. The pine martens were progressively eliminated from most English counties and from Wales, although a few scattered individuals may have survived, even into the late 20th century.

With legal protection and fewer gamekeepers, the pine marten has recolonized parts of Scotland and may also establish itself in northern England once again. Recovery has been assisted by large-scale planting of conifer forests for commercial timber production. The forests not only provide the preferred habitat for pine martens but also, in their early stages of growth, support huge numbers of voles, the pine martens' favorite food.

## DATA PANEL

**Pine marten**

*Martes martes*

**Family:** Mustelidae

**World population:** Probably over 200,000

**Distribution:** Most of Europe, from Spain to western Siberia, but scarce in many places

**Habitat:** Temperate pine forests up to the treeline; dens made in hollow trees and cavities in rocks

**Size:** Length head/body: 14–22 in (36–56 cm); tail: 7–11 in (17–28 cm); height at shoulder: 6 in (15 cm); female at least 10–12% smaller than male. Weight: 1.1–4.5 lb (0.5–2.2 kg)

**Form:** A long, thin cat-sized animal, with chocolate-brown fur, a bushy tail, and creamy-orange throat patch

**Diet:** Small mammals, particularly voles, but also birds, insects, and even seashore animals; sometimes ripe fruit

**Breeding:** One litter a year; usually 3 (but up to 6) young in each; mature at 14 months. Life span about 10–15 years; maximum 18 in captivity

**Related endangered species:** European mink *(Mustela lutreola)*\* EN; various otters and other mustelids

**Status:** Not listed by IUCN; not listed by CITES

**See also:** Reintroduction **1:** 92; Ferret, Black-Footed **4:** 72; Mink, European **6:** 78; Otter, European **7:** 32

## Changing Attitudes

Gamekeepers today are better informed about the habits of pine martens and therefore more tolerant of them. On the European continent gamekeepers were less vigorous in their extermination of the animals, so the species has remained more numerous there. Major threats now facing pine martens include busy roads and predation by eagle owls; some farmers also poison or trap the animals to protect their chickens.

In the early part of the 20th century pine marten numbers were severely depleted by the fur industry. The animal's coat was highly prized, and many thousands of pine martens were killed every year to satisfy demand. In some places commercial harvesting continues, although in Russia there has been an 80 percent drop in numbers caught since the 1920s, when pine martens were more abundant, and their fur was considered to be the height of fashion.

**The pine marten**

*is a tree-dwelling member of the weasel family. Pine martens have been hunted heavily for their fur. They were also killed as a result of gamekeepers' efforts to eliminate predators.*

**75**

# Mesite, White-Breasted

### Mesitornis variegata

*The strange and little-known white-breasted mesite of Madagascar is found in only a handful of widely separated locations. The population is forecast to suffer a rapid decline in the near future.*

Mesites (sometimes known as roatelos) are an odd family with just three living species, all found only on the island of Madagascar. In the past they have been classified with the gamebirds, rails, pigeons, and even perching birds or placed in an order of their own. Today most ornithologists think that the mesites belong within the order Gruiformes, along with the rails, cranes, bustards, and others.

Left behind when Madagascar split off and drifted away from the great mass of the African continent over 65 million years ago, they are often thought to be a primitive group of birds. All three species are threatened today, and all are classified as Vulnerable.

The white-breasted mesite only became known to science in 1834, and this first record was not tied to a precise locality. Almost a century was to pass until the next bird was found in the Ankarafantsika Forest, now known to be one of its strongholds. It was rediscovered here in the 1980s after being unrecorded for over 50 years. The species has an odd distribution, with populations known from only five sites in northern and western Madagascar and one in the east. Surveys confirm that it does not occur between these areas, despite apparently suitable habitat—deciduous forest with dense overhead cover, an herb layer clear of dead branches, and deep leaf litter.

Pairs of white-breasted mesites live as family groups with the young of the previous breeding season. Like the other species of mesites, they are strictly ground-dwellers; and although they can fly, they rarely do so. They gather food mainly from the layer of leaf litter carpeting the forest floor, but also sometimes from low vegetation. Their distinctive feeding style involves flicking aside dead leaves with their strong bills to expose their food—small insects, other invertebrates, and seeds.

## Declining Populations

With its dark and light patterned plumage providing excellent disruptive camouflage against the dappled light of the forest floor and its skulking habits, the white-breasted mesite is most easily counted by playing tapes of its songs and listening for replies. Males utter a series of loud, melodic whistles and often duet with their partners to proclaim ownership of their territory. These joint performances, lasting up to a minute, take the form of a perfectly coordinated series of whistles from the male alternating with the female's stuttering notes, becoming louder and louder.

Such censuses have indicated a total population of about 8,000 birds at the two main sites, some 6,000 at Ankarafantsika and 2,000 in the Menabe area. Although the numbers may seem quite high, the density and breeding success of the birds in these areas appeared to be poor, and populations at the sites in the far north and the single east coast site may represent isolated remnants.

## Threats

The species occurs at its highest densities and breeds most successfully in sites near rivers—the areas of forest that are the most favored for logging and subsistence slash-and-burn agriculture. Although conservation programs are in place at four of the five western and northern sites, the future of Ankarafantsika and Analamera as reserves is not assured. Also, illegal logging and slash-and-burn cultivation, grass fires, and exploitation of the area for

**See also:** Populations **1:** 20; Saving the Habitats **1:** 88; Corncrake **3:** 66

## DATA PANEL

**White-breasted mesite (white-breasted roatelo)**

*Mesitornis variegata*

**Family:** Mesitornithidae

**World population:** About 8,000 birds

**Distribution:** Madagascar; recorded at a few sites in the north, west, and only 1 in the east

**Habitat:** Dry, deciduous forests near rivers (in south) or on sand (in north); one record from rain forest (in east)

**Size:** Length: 12.3 in (31 cm); wingspan: not recorded. Weight: 3.6–4 oz (103–111 g)

**Form:** Smaller than town pigeon, with smallish head and shortish, straight, gray bill; large, broad, rounded tail and thick undertail feathers; short, rounded wings and sturdy legs; head whitish, boldly marked with a reddish-brown crown and 2 broad stripes; ring of grayish to blue bare skin around eye; upperparts, wings, and tail reddish brown apart from variable grayish patch on nape; underparts pale cream with scattered black crescents on lower breast sides and narrow reddish-brown bars with blackish mottling on belly

**Diet:** Mainly small insects and their larvae; other invertebrates, including cockroaches, crickets, beetles, spiders, and centipedes; also seeds, especially in the dry season

**Breeding:** Nests October–April in a loose platform of sticks in shrub layer; female lays 2–3 whitish eggs and incubates them for an unknown period

**Related endangered species:** Brown mesite (*Mesitornis unicolor*) VU; subdesert mesite (*Monias benschi*) VU

**Status:** IUCN VU; not listed by CITES

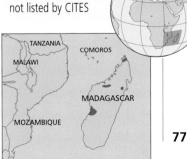

firewood or charcoal all continue to threaten the mesites' already fragmented habitat.

Hunting poses an additional threat and is increasing as logging and other developments open up new areas. Although the fairly small mesites are not usually targeted by hunters, when they are flushed out by dogs, they are considered tasty quarry. Despite such threats, provided that effective conservation of the west's dry forests can be achieved, there is still hope for the enigmatic mesite.

**The white-breasted mesite** *uses its long bill to feed in various ways, including searching beneath leaves for prey, thrashing rolled-up dead leaves against the ground to dislodge invertebrates, and digging in soil for seeds.*

# Mink, European

## Mustela lutreola

*Once widespread in Europe, native mink populations are now in rapid decline. The animal's future is under threat both from humans and from the introduced American mink.*

Like its American cousin, the European mink inhabits waterside habitats and is found along river banks and at the edges of lakes. It is mainly nocturnal, operating out of a burrow or natural den among tree roots. Some take over burrows made by water voles, but a mink can dig its own home if necessary. Mink are territorial and normally live alone: They tend to be well spaced out, with an average of only one mink per mile of river bank. They swim and dive well, aided by their partly webbed feet, and capture most of their food in the water. They also hunt on land, using their sense of smell to track down small rodents, frogs, and other prey.

Only a century ago the European mink was found across northern Europe and in parts of northern Asia. It has been extinct in most of western Europe for decades and is now also extinct in eastern European countries such as Lithuania, probably also in Finland and Poland. It remains widespread in Russia, where over 95 percent of the surviving populations live, but their distribution and exact status are uncertain.

Reasons for their decline include eager hunting and trapping for their valuable fur. Mink are easy to catch, so the temptation to overharvest them has not been resisted, and their slow breeding rate has been unable to compensate for heavy losses. Females produce up to seven young but only once a year and the survival rate is often low. Kittens are raised without help from the male and are independent at about 10 weeks. Some disperse 30 miles (50 km) or more, especially in winter, when it may be necessary to travel such distances to find unfrozen water.

### Man-Made Hazards

Mink face other problems, including water pollution. They have also been affected by habitat loss, since many rivers have been dammed to provide electricity or modified to prevent floods and allow cultivation of land along their edges. Even in relatively undisturbed areas such as Belarus recent surveys show the mink has been declining. In

## DATA PANEL

**European mink**

*Mustela lutreola*

**Family:** Mustelidae

**World population:** 30,000–40,000

**Distribution:** Belarus, Estonia, France, Georgia, Latvia, Spain, and widely in Russia

**Habitat:** River banks near temperate grassland

**Size:** Length head/body: 12–18 in (30–45 cm); tail: 4.5–7.5 in (12–19 cm). Weight: 1.3–1.75 lb (550–800 g)

**Form:** Small mammal resembling a small, short-legged cat; dark, glossy, brown fur with white around muzzle

**Diet:** Rodents, including water voles and muskrats, small birds, and aquatic invertebrates such as crayfish and mollusks

**Breeding:** Breeding season February–March; 4–7 young born April–June; 1 litter a year. Life span 7–10 years

**Related endangered species:** Wolverine (*Gulo gulo*)* VU; Colombian weasel (*Mustela felipei*) EN; pine marten (*Martes martes*)* O; giant otter (*Pteronura brasiliensis*)* EN

**Status:** IUCN EN; not listed by CITES

**See also:** Drainage and Irrigation **1:** 40; Introductions **1:** 54; Ferret, Black-Footed **4:** 72; Otter, European **7:** 32

addition to this, in 1926 American mink were imported into Europe to be reared on fur farms. Many of them escaped and now compete directly with their smaller European cousin for food, dens, and living space. It is also said that male American mink can mate successfully with female European mink. However, although the babies begin to develop, they never survive. Since mink have only one litter a year, crossbreeding means that female European mink waste a whole year's reproductive effort.

It appears that the American species is a more successful survivor, and in under 75 years it has spread throughout Scandinavia, much of Britain, and the Netherlands. Other populations are also spreading rapidly in France, Spain, Italy, and Germany. In places where both species of mink occur together, the European mink seems to die out within five to 10 years.

In 1992 a special breeding program for the European mink was established with the aim of maintaining a viable population in captivity. In 1997 there were 64 individuals in 10 zoos. In the wild the decline continues at an alarming rate, and the native wild mink seems destined to become extinct in western Europe. Efforts are being made to establish populations on offshore islands, safe from the dangers on the mainland.

**The European mink** *is smaller than its American cousin. Only 2 to 3 percent of the remaining population live in Europe. This one has matted fur, having just left the water.*

# Mole, Marsupial

## Notoryctes typhlops

*Of all Australia's mammals, the marsupial moles of the western desert are certainly among the more unusual species. Since they normally spend almost their entire lives buried in the sandy soil, they are also among the least well understood.*

Before declaring an animal Endangered, the IUCN normally needs convincing scientific evidence that the species is likely to become extinct unless the causes of the declining numbers are removed. In most cases the evidence for a species' decline is not difficult to come by—we can often easily see there are fewer individuals than there once were. Occasionally, however, there are exceptions; in the case of the marsupial moles of Australia the IUCN agreed to classify the species as Endangered even though most scientists who have tried to study the species admit that they have no idea how many marsupial moles there may be.

Marsupial moles are extraordinary for many reasons. In lifestyle and appearance they are very similar to African golden moles; but other than the fact that both are mammals, they are only distantly related. The similarities are a stunning example of what biologists call convergent evolution, where two completely different types of animal evolve into very similar forms because it is the best way of dealing with similar challenges of habitat or way of life. In the case of the marsupial mole the challenge is how to live buried in the desert sand.

### Two of a Kind

The marsupial mole (sometimes also called the southern marsupial mole) has been known about since the 19th century. However, individuals are rarely seen—which is not surprising given the animal's way of life. In 1920 a new sort of marsupial mole was discovered close to Eighty Mile Beach on the northwestern coast of Western Australia. This variety, called the northern marsupial mole, was a little smaller than the southern marsupial mole, and it had a differently shaped nose-shield and tail.

Whether the northern marsupial mole qualifies as a separate species is the subject of a debate that is unlikely to be resolved, since the animals are so hard to find. However, from time to time specimens of the southern marsupial mole are discovered. People finding the moles are usually puzzled enough to contact a museum or university, and dead or dying specimens have been collected at a rate of five to 15 animals every 10 years.

The real challenge is to find and study a living marsupial mole of the northern variety. Scientists

---

### DATA PANEL

**Marsupial mole (southern marsupial mole)**

***Notoryctes typhlops***

**Family:** Notoryctidae

**World population:** Unknown and almost impossible to estimate

**Distribution:** Northwestern Australia

**Habitat:** Desert burrows

**Size:** Length head/body: 4–6 in (10–16 cm); tail: 1 in (2.4 cm). Weight: 1.2–2.5 oz (35–70 g)

**Form:** Flat-bodied animal with pale-golden fur; very short legs; spadelike front feet; no functional eyes, ear hole hidden in fur; nose has tough, horny shield, tail short and stubby. Female has a pouch opening to rear

**Diet:** Insect grubs, particularly larvae of beetles and moths

**Breeding:** Unknown

**Related endangered species:** Northern marsupial mole *(Notoryctes caurinus)* EN, although it may not qualify as a separate species. Its scientific classification is the subject of a debate

**Status:** IUCN EN; not listed by CITES

AUSTRALIA

have spent years searching the deserts, enlisting the support of local people living in remote Aboriginal communities. In 1998 two schoolboys found and captured a living specimen of the northern marsupial mole, which ended up at the Museum of Western Australia. It did not adapt to life in captivity and died after about eight weeks, having not eaten well in all that time.

Marsupial moles do occasionally come to the surface, usually after rain. When they emerge, their bodies leave distinctive furrows in the sand, with marks either side where they have used their legs to haul themselves along. Further proof that the moles are around can be found by taking core samples of firm sand and looking for the oval-shaped areas of looser material that show a mole has passed through. Scientists have tried burying sound-sensitive microphones in the sand to detect passing moles. The problem with all such techniques is that, while they show that there are moles around, they do not give any idea how many there are. Until researchers can get some idea about population size, it is very difficult to prove what position the species is in.

There is no shortage of goodwill toward the moles, since they do not appear to damage human activities such as farming. They have been killed out of curiosity or for their silky fur, but are not deliberately hunted. The marsupial moles' chief problem is likely to be changes in their habitat due to controlled burning of bush and grass to create grazing pastures. Predation by introduced species, such as cats, could be a problem too. A high proportion of fox droppings have been found to contain marsupial mole remains, thus proving that the marsupial mole's predators are better at finding them than people are.

**The marsupial mole** *has fine, sandy-colored silky fur and shovellike hands, which it uses to "swim" through sand. It can be found up to 5 feet (1.5 m) below the surface. It has no eyes or obvious ears, which would quickly clog with sand, and the female's pouch opens toward the rear, so it does not get full of sand.*

# Mole-Rat, Balkans

### *Spalax graecus*

*Often exterminated as pests, several mole-rat species have been reduced to small, scattered populations. The Balkans mole-rat is at risk from urban development and modern farming.*

Mole-rats are rodents and do not have the big digging "hands" of true moles. Instead, they use the incisor teeth that are characteristic of all rodents, but which in mole-rats are hugely enlarged. The teeth are permanently exposed, but the mole-rat's lips can close behind them to prevent earth from getting into the mouth.

Like true moles, mole-rats are highly specialized for burrowing. They have no eyes, and their tiny ears are buried in short, dense fur. The burrows they create are extensive and often quite elaborate, incorporating special food-storage chambers. The tunnels are usually situated close to the surface, but can descend more than 5 feet (1.5 m) underground.

When digging in the burrows, a mole-rat pushes the excavated earth up into small hills or "tumps." One hill will be bigger than the rest and is built to cover the animal's nest chamber. The nest consists of a ball of grass or other dry vegetation in which the young are born early in the year.

## A Solitary Life Underground

Mole-rats are solitary animals, and each has its own private tunnel system. They are nocturnal and rarely come to the surface. However, they must come out of their burrows sometimes, since their remains turn up among the prey of owls from time to time. The predators' victims are probably for the most part young animals moving away from their mothers' tunnels. When underground, the mole-rats are normally safe from predators and so do not need to be prolific breeders to compensate for large numbers being killed by carnivorous mammals and birds.

The low birthrate, however, makes the population vulnerable if large numbers are lost due to other causes. The problem confronting the mole-rats today is that their digging and feeding activities make them a nuisance to farmers. They feed mainly on roots, sometimes causing considerable damage to crops such as potatoes and carrots. Their tunneling also disturbs other crops, affecting plant growth and reducing yields in arable areas. The mole-rat's activities also cause problems in forestry plantations, damaging the growing trees.

Mole-rats often feed by pulling plant material down into the burrows, a typical sign of their

## DATA PANEL

**Balkans mole-rat**

*Spalax graecus*

**Family:** Muridae

**World population:** Thousands, but scattered

**Distribution:** Romania and Ukraine

**Habitat:** Steppes, dry grassland, and small fields

**Size:** Length: 6–10.5 in (15–27 cm). Weight: 5–8 oz (140–220 g)

**Form:** Thickset, molelike rodent with no tail, tiny ears, and huge incisor teeth

**Diet:** Roots and plant material dragged into burrow system

**Breeding:** Breeds in early spring, producing 1 litter of usually 2–4 young per year. Life span unknown, but probably up to 4 years

**Related endangered species:** Closest relatives include *Spalax arenarius* (no common name), *S. giganteus* (no common name), and *S. micropthalmus*, all of which are listed as Vulnerable

**Status:** IUCN VU; not listed by CITES

[Map showing: SLOVAKIA, HUNGARY, UKRAINE, MOLDOVA, ROMANIA, YUGOSLAVIA, BULGARIA]

presence. The plant material is then eaten in safety or stored in special chambers in the tunnel system. The mole-rat's foraging habits can prove costly to farmers, who often respond by trapping or poisoning the animals at every opportunity. Deliberate killing of mole-rats is localized, however, and probably does not seriously affect the population over wide areas.

## Growing Pressures

The greatest threat to the mole-rat's long-term survival comes from modern plowing practices. Ancient plows, particularly the traditional, wooden, ox-drawn variety, only scratched the surface of the soil. However, modern, tractor-drawn plows turn the soil over to a depth of more than 15 inches (38 cm). In so doing, they dig deep into the soft, dry undersoil, destroying the mole-rat's nests and burrow systems. The effect can be to eradicate mole-rats over large areas. Modern machinery is used to enlarge fields and removes patches of bush and other vegetation under which the mole-rats might otherwise seek refuge.

Urban development, including the spread of roads, the expansion of towns, and the building of more houses and gardens, has also fragmented or removed substantial areas of the grassland habitat in which the mole-rats used to occur. As a result, several species have become locally extinct across large areas of southeastern Europe and the Middle East. Elsewhere, the remaining populations are now scattered and in danger of being destroyed one by one.

Since mole-rats are not used to dispersing over long distances, they have no way of escaping from the relentless destruction of their habitat by development. They are also ill equipped to recolonize areas from which they have been displaced. As a result, the Balkans mole-rat is now becoming scarce. There appears to be no sign of any reprieve in the pressures affecting the mole-rat, and its Vulnerable status indicates a growing concern for the species.

**The Balkans mole-rat** *digs with its teeth, while true moles use their enlarged hands.*

# Mole-Rat, Giant

*Tachyoryctes macrocephalus*

*The giant mole-rat is an inhabitant of the harsh, remote Ethiopian highlands. Little is known about the species, but it is clear that it faces increased competition from domestic grazing animals.*

The giant mole-rat is an example of a species that may well be close to extinction or alternatively may be perfectly safe. We simply do not know because it has hardly ever been studied by scientists. The species was first described in 1842 by a German explorer who based his report on a single skin from an unknown locality. The animal was next reported in 1900 in the Bale Mountains in Ethiopia, but was forgotten again for the next half century. It was rediscovered in the 1960s, and the first ecological observations were made in the mid-1970s.

Giant mole-rats appear to be confined to the high moorland plateau of the Bale Mountains, where they live at altitudes of up to 13,600 feet (4,150 m). They are rabbit sized and therefore much larger than the common mole-rats found at lower altitudes elsewhere in Africa. At these heights the nights are often extremely cold, especially during the dry season, when the skies are clear. During the day, however, the air is quite warm, and the sun can heat the surface of the ground to 75°F (23°C).

In such conditions the mole-rats only come out during the day. They keep a watchful lookout for predators, particularly the Ethiopian wolf, buzzards, and various other birds of prey. The mole-rats' eyes are placed high up on the skull, so they do not need to come far out of their burrows in order to scrutinize the skies above. If the coast is clear, they emerge a little farther to gather food, without ever venturing more than halfway out into the open. Instead, they quickly scrape together all the green foliage within reach and drag it back underground. The mole-rats pick out the choice morsels in the safety of the tunnel and then push the rest back to the surface to form a heap of plant debris.

When the food resources around one burrow entrance are exhausted—usually in less than 20 minutes—they extend the tunnel farther to collect more food. In the late afternoon they plug all the exits with soil to keep out the cold night air. The mole-rats are so wary that they seem to spend less than an hour a day at the surface.

### Competition in a Limited Range

The giant mole-rat's tunnels seem to be interconnected and may be shared by two or more animals. In places large numbers of giant mole-rats can occupy a small area of ground—perhaps as many as 12,500 per square mile (5,000 per sq. km). The

## DATA PANEL

**Giant mole-rat**

*Tachyoryctes macrocephalus*

**Family:** Rhizomyidae

**World population:** Unknown

**Distribution:** Bale Mountains, southeastern Ethiopia

**Habitat:** High-altitude moorland above 10,000 ft (3,000 m)

**Size:** Length head/body: 6.7–12.3 in (17–31.3 cm); tail: 1.4–2.6 in (3.5–6.5 cm). Weight: 5–32 oz (40–930 g)

**Form:** Short-legged, thickset animal with soft, yellowish-brown fur and huge orange incisor teeth. Tiny ears and eyes

**Diet:** Green vegetation

**Breeding:** Unknown

**Related endangered species:** King mole-rat (*Tachyoryctes rex*) EN; Naivasha mole-rat (*T. naivashae*) EN; mianzini mole-rat (*T. annectens*) EN; audacious mole-rat (*T. audax*) VU; Ankole mole-rat (*T. ankoliae*) VU; Balkans mole-rat (*Spalax leucodon*)* VU

**Status:** Not listed by IUCN; not listed by CITES

**See also:** Biomes **1:** 18; Pasture **1:** 38; Mole-Rat, Balkans **6:** 82

problem for the species is that only a limited area is available to it. Mole-rats need deep soil in which to dig their tunnels, but much of their mountain habitat consists of rocky slopes. Parts of the mountain plateau where they live are also wet and unsuitable for burrowing. Consequently, populations live mainly in the wide valleys and not on the rocky ridges in between. Each valley and patch of suitable habitat has its own separate population, and the animals probably do not mix very much, since they hardly ever leave their burrows.

In the past these high-altitude moorlands were uninhabited, but farmers have since settled in the area. Livestock, including herds of goats and cattle, tramples the ground and grazes on the vegetation needed by the giant mole-rats. Domestic dogs have also been added to the animal's list of potential predators. The additional activity from humans and animals can only have the effect of discouraging the cautious mole-rats from emerging from their burrows, further reducing the time available to them for gathering food.

The giant mole-rats enjoy one major advantage over their lowland-dwelling cousins: Their high-altitude habitat remains unsuitable for cultivation, which has caused the extinction of mole-rats in Europe and the Middle East. However, other species of *Tachyoryctes* are already endangered elsewhere in Africa, and in time the same fate may still befall the largest species of all in Ethiopia.

**The giant mole-rat,** *unlike other* Tachyoryctes *species (often called root rats elsewhere in Africa), seems to depend on surface vegetation rather than on roots for its food. Consequently, it will be more affected by competition from domestic grazers as they become more numerous in the Ethiopian mountains.*

# Monkey, Douc

*Pygathrix nemaeus*

*One of the world's most colorful primates, the douc monkey faces a highly uncertain future in its native Indochina. Generations of environmental destruction, hunting, and collection for the pet trade are largely responsible for the animal's decline.*

Two hundred years ago the populations of doúc monkeys encountered by early European visitors were such easy prey that one report, from 1819, tells of a hunting party that went ashore at Da Nang in Vietnam and killed over 100 doucs before breakfast. The doucs apparently had no fear of gunfire—in fact, quite the opposite. Doucs from the surrounding area actually came closer to the hunters to investigate the noise. The story creates the impression of a bold, curious, and common animal, a far cry from the situation in more recent times. When scientists went back to the same area in 1974, they found fewer than 40 doucs in 10 weeks; now the Da Nang population seems to have disappeared.

The few remaining wild populations of douc monkey have not been well studied. The species was virtually unknown before 1967, when the first scientific observations were made. The outbreak of the Vietnam War prevented serious study for many years. The war was not only devastating in human terms, it also laid to waste huge areas of forest. Fires burned out of control, and trees were torn apart by bombs and bullets and poisoned by chemicals. There is little doubt that thousands of monkeys were killed; many may have been hunted and eaten by troops camping in the forest.

## Survival

The problems facing doucs today are more ordinary, but no less serious. Large areas of forest are constantly being felled for timber or cleared to make way for agriculture or human settlement. The monkeys are still

---

### DATA PANEL

**Douc monkey (douc langur, cochin, China monkey)**

*Pygathrix nemaeus*

**Family:** Cercopithecidae

**World population:** Unknown

**Distribution:** Cambodia, Laos, and Vietnam

**Habitat:** Tropical rain forest and monsoon forest up to 6,560 ft (2,000 m) above sea level

**Size:** Length head/body: 24–30 in (61–76 cm); tail: 22–30 in (56–76 cm); males about 20% bigger than females. Weight: 17.6–24.2 lb (8–11 kg)

**Form:** Dramatically marked monkey; red-brown head, gray back, white rump, tail, and forearms; black upper arms, hands, legs, and feet; yellow or black face, depending on subspecies

**Diet:** Leaves and fruit

**Breeding:** One, rarely 2, young born February–June after gestation of 6–7 months; mature at 4–5 years (females breed earlier than males). Life span over 25 years

**Related endangered species:** Grizzled leaf monkey (*Presbytis comata*) EN; proboscis monkey (*Nasalis larvatus*)* EN; Guizhou snub-nosed monkey (*Rhinopithecus brelichi*) EN; pig-tailed snub-nosed monkey (*Simias concolor*) EN

**Status:** IUCN EN; CITES I

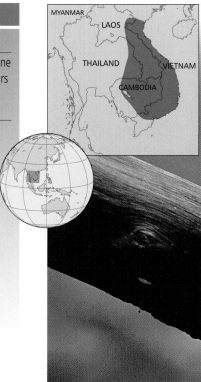

---

**See also:** War **1:** 47; The Role of Zoos **1:** 86; Monkey, Proboscis **6:** 90; Macaque, Japanese **6:** 56

hunted for meat and captured for the illegal pet trade.

With its luxurious "coat of many colors," few mammals match the striking appearance of the douc. Combine its dramatic looks with a typical monkey personality, and it is not difficult to see why the animals make excellent pets. However, no true animal lover would want to keep an animal at the expense of driving it to extinction in the wild. Collecting for the pet trade may now be the most important factor in the douc's continuing decline, largely because the majority of monkeys taken from the wild die soon after capture, never making it to the pet dealer, let alone to a new home.

Before 1991 there were thought to be two species of douc monkey, known as the red-shanked and black-shanked doucs. They differed slightly in color and markings, and came from different areas: the red-shanked

from the north and the black-shanked from the south of Vietnam. The two are now classed as a single species, but the remaining wild populations are little studied. They live in much smaller troops than before: Early reports describe groups of 30 to 50 doucs living together, but recently observed groups rarely exceed 15 individuals. There are several douc monkeys in zoos, but they do not teach us much about the lives of doucs in the wild. Nevertheless, the captive population may serve as an important reserve should the situation in the wild get worse.

*The douc monkey is a dramatic-looking animal, with contrasting patches of black, white, chestnut-red, and gray fur. The different colored varieties found in the north and south of the range were once thought to be separate species.*

# Monkey, Goeldi's

*Callimico goeldii*

*One of the rarest primates of South America, the unique Goeldi's monkey is little understood and poses several interesting questions for zoologists. It is feared that the species may be extinct before many of these questions can be answered.*

Goeldi's monkey has never been a common animal, mainly because it specializes in living in dense, scrubby forest habitat that is naturally patchy in South America. The species is therefore divided up into small, isolated populations, each restricted to its own island of habitat. In ecological terms such isolation is a recipe for rarity; it is no surprise that Goeldi's monkey was one of the last of the South American primates to be discovered—it was not found until 1904.

The rarity of Goeldi's monkey has hindered efforts to study it in the field, although it has been successfully bred in a number of zoos around the world. However, enough is known about the biology of the monkey to have created a prolonged scientific debate about its relationship with other species. In many ways Goeldi's monkey seems to be an intermediate between the two main families of South American primates: the Callitrichidae (tamarins and marmosets) and the Cebidae (capuchinlike monkeys, sometimes called New World monkeys). It shares some physical features with each family, and despite its alternative name—Goeldi's marmoset—it is often classified as a tamarin or put into its own family, the Callimiconidae.

One important difference between Goeldi's monkey and the other tamarins and marmosets is its breeding biology. While the other species tend to give birth to twins, female Goeldi's monkeys only have one baby each time. In addition, only one female in a group breeds at a time. Most of the other females (usually her older daughters) help look after the baby by carrying it and bringing it food. The young monkey is extremely well cared for and stands a good chance of surviving into adulthood. Indeed, the system may seem like the perfect example of animals playing "happy families." However, the drawback is that numbers increase slowly, and the population takes a long time to recover from losses, even where there is enough available habitat.

## Clearing the Forest

While nobody knows how many Goeldi's monkeys are left in the wild, there is little doubt that habitat destruction is threatening the species with extinction.

---

## DATA PANEL

**Goeldi's monkey (Goeldi's marmoset, callimico)**

*Callimico goeldii*

**Family:** Callitrichidae

**World population:** Unknown

**Distribution:** Rain forests of Colombia, eastern Peru, western Brazil, and northern Bolivia; possibly eastern Ecuador

**Habitat:** Open-canopied rain forest with dense understory of scrub

**Size:** Length head/body: 7–12 in (18–31 cm); tail: 10–12.5 in (25–32 cm). Weight: 14–30 oz (400–860 g)

**Form:** Small monkey; silky, dark-brown or black fur, longer on neck and shoulders; sometimes white markings on face; fingers and toes (except big toe) have tough claws

**Diet:** Mostly fruit; also insects and small animals

**Breeding:** Single young born at any time of year after gestation of 5–6 months; fully weaned at 12 weeks; mature at 14 months. May live up to 18 years in captivity

**Related endangered species:** Many other marmosets and tamarins, including golden-white tassel-ear marmoset (*Callithrix flaviceps*) VU; black-headed marmoset (*C. nigriceps*) VU; golden-rumped tamarin (*Leontophithecus chrysopygus*) CR; white-footed tamarin (*Saguinus leucopus*) VU

**Status:** IUCN VU; CITES I

---

**See also:** Speciation 1: 26; Captive Breeding 1: 87; Tamarin, Golden Lion 9: 52

Where forest has been cleared for agriculture, there are reports of Goeldi's monkeys emerging from the scrub to raid cocoa plantations, but in general the species is so rare that most people in its native countries have never heard of it, let alone seen one. In the absence of information conservation is difficult. For example, while the setting aside of areas of forest for nature reserves is useful, it is difficult for conservationists to know which areas should be the highest priority for preservation without detailed knowledge of the monkey's habitat preferences.

## Captive Populations

Goeldi's monkeys seem to take well to life in captivity, so long as they are allowed to live in natural family groups. There are currently about 450 individuals living in captive populations around the world. Most zoos are cooperating in an international breeding plan, coordinated by the Chicago Zoo. Detailed records are kept, and breeding takes place between monkeys from different zoos to make sure that the captive populations do not suffer too much from inbreeding.

Not enough is known about the habitat requirements of Goeldi's monkey to carry out reintroduction programs, but the captive population may yet prove to be a valuable reserve.

**Goeldi's monkeys** *are characterized by their black silky fur and mane of thick hair on the neck and shoulders. The species is so rare that even in its native countries, most people would not recognize one if they saw it in the wild.*

# Monkey, Proboscis

### *Nasalis larvatus*

*The proboscis monkey was once fortunate enough to live in one of the world's most inaccessible and undisturbed areas. Today, despite government protection, the species is endangered because of destruction of its mangrove forest habitat.*

Until quite recently the extraordinary-looking proboscis monkey was relatively common on its native island of Borneo. Even while other native primates—such as the orang-utan—were suffering dramatic population declines, the proboscis monkey appeared to be holding its own. The main reason for its success was its inaccessible habitat; the species lives in some of the most impenetrable places on the island, namely, the dense mangrove forests that once lined many of the region's rivers. Mangroves form a dense mass of branches and stems, standing in water and soft mud. It is virtually impossible to walk around in mangrove thickets, which may extend unbroken for many miles. Animals living there are fairly safe and have adapted to climb and scramble around with ease. While the stable rain forest of Borneo's interior was being felled for timber and wood pulp, or cleared for agriculture, the mangroves remained inaccessible to machinery, and the space they occupied was unsuitable for agriculture. The waterlogged forest had little commercial value and was left to the proboscis monkeys and other specialized mangrove wildlife.

## A Life Near Water

Proboscis monkeys are the most aquatic of all the primates. Their partially webbed feet make them excellent swimmers, and they sometimes use the water as a convenient emergency escape route. Alarmed monkeys will readily plunge 50 feet (15 m) from a treetop to the relative safety of the water. Such a jump onto dry land would result in serious injury, even for an agile primate.

The monkeys tend not to feed in the water, surviving instead on a diet of leaves plucked from the trees. The leaves are generally tough and not nutritious, so they have to be eaten in large quantities. It has been estimated that the contents of an adult proboscis monkey's stomach accounts for about a quarter of its body weight. The huge meals pass slowly through the monkey's digestive system and are broken down by special gut-dwelling bacteria. The bacteria also break down some of the toxic chemicals produced by mangroves and many other forest plants,

## DATA PANEL

**Proboscis monkey**

***Nasalis larvatus***

**Family:** Cercopithecidae

**World population:** About 260,000 (1986 estimate); now likely to be considerably fewer

**Distribution:** Borneo

**Habitat:** Freshwater mangrove and lowland rain forest

**Size:** Length head/body: 21–30 in (53–76 cm); tail: 22–30 in (56–76 cm); males twice as big as females. Weight: 17–30 lb (7–22 kg)

**Form:** Large, long-tailed monkey with variable red-brown fur that fades to white on underside. Feet partially webbed. Nose is small and snub in juveniles and females; large and pendulous in males

**Diet:** Mostly leaves of pedada trees; some fruit seeds; also flowers

**Breeding:** Single young born at any time of year after 24-week gestation. Life span unknown; probably at least 10 years

**Related endangered species:** No close relatives, but at least 35 other species of Old World monkey family Cercopithecidae are classified as Vulnerable or Endangered

**Status:** IUCN EN; CITES I

**See also:** Island Biogeography **1:** 30; Drainage and Irrigation **1:** 40; Monkey, Douc **6:** 86

enabling the proboscis monkey to take advantage of food that other animals have to avoid.

## A Nose for Success

The large nose of the mature male proboscis monkey is what gives the species its name, but its precise purpose is unknown. Being much larger than females, males are more prone to overheating: One theory is that the nose acts as a cooling device, radiating excess body heat. It may also be that the large nose is a badge of success, since it continues to grow throughout a male's life; the males with the largest noses are the oldest and presumably, therefore, the fittest and most successful breeders. In choosing a suitable male to father her offspring, a female may use the size of a male's nose as an indicator of his genetic desirability.

## Reduced Circumstances

It would be a tragedy if proboscis monkey numbers were reduced by so much that the species became more famous for being rare than for its other unique characteristics. However, its future is uncertain. The mangroves that provide its home are now harvested for wood, and modern drainage technology has meant that the watery world of the proboscis monkey is being invaded by developers. The rivers that once flooded the forests—creating natural refuges for wildlife—have been tamed, and in just a few decades well over half of Borneo's mangrove forest has disappeared. Previously extensive mangrove swamps have been reduced to narrow fringes along rivers and no longer supply adequate habitat for the monkeys.

There are a few proboscis monkeys in captivity. However, the species is considered difficult to keep in zoos, perhaps because it is not easy to re-create its natural mangrove habitat in artificial conditions. With the entire wild population confined to one island, the priority must be the preservation of its habitat.

**The male proboscis monkey's** *extraordinary nose makes it one of the most easily recognized of all primates. Females and youngsters have small, upturned noses.*

# Mouse, St. Kilda

*Apodemus sylvaticus hirtensis*

*The St. Kilda mouse is typical of many subspecies of small mammals that form tiny populations in remote places and are highly vulnerable, being found nowhere else in the world.*

The St. Kilda mouse does not face any particular threats. However, it is found only on the tiny island of Hirta in the North Atlantic and perhaps one other of the St. Kilda archipelago. These windswept, precipitous islands lie 40 miles (65 km) from the most westerly of Scotland's Outer Hebrides. Hirta was only occupied by the British Army, which had a missile range there. It is now a nature reserve.

If there were a major natural disaster on Hirta, the mice could disappear, and they may die out anyway through inbreeding for many generations. Visitors may carry rats, dogs, or cats, to the island, a serious threat to island mammals. Fortunately, this never happened during the time that the island was occupied.

However, the St. Kilda mouse population remains small and highly vulnerable. It is typical of many island races of small mammals (and other animals) that have become stranded in remote places and undergone their own process of private evolution until they no longer resemble the mainland forms from which they are descended.

The St. Kilda mouse is derived from the common wood mouse, which is found widely on the mainland of Britain and Europe. We know that the St. Kilda mouse must have arrived quite recently and evolved rapidly (within a few centuries at most) on its remote island home because at the end of the Ice Age (10,000 years ago) the islands were still covered by solid ice. The deep sea surrounding St. Kilda means that the mice could only have got there with human help. They must have been transported accidentally among thatching materials or supplies of food carried from the mainland.

Studies of skull similarities suggest that the original wood mice reached St. Kilda over 1,000 years ago and that they arrived from Scandinavia, not the nearest parts of mainland Scotland. They were probably carried to St. Kilda by the Vikings during their famous voyages. The islands have no mammalian predators and no other small mammals

## DATA PANEL

**St. Kilda mouse**

***Apodemus sylvaticus hirtensis***

**Family:** Muridae

**World population:** About 1,000

**Distribution:** Outer Hebridean island of Hirta, St. Kilda group, off the west coast of Scotland

**Habitat:** Windswept, grassy slopes; in ruined buildings

**Size:** Length head/body: 4.5–5 in (11–13 cm); tail: 3–4 in (8–10 cm). Weight: 1.4–1.8 oz (40–50 g)

**Form:** Brownish above, creamy-gray below; large eyes and long tail. Coat thicker and woollier than in mainland mice

**Diet:** Plants, insects, and seeds

**Breeding:** About 6–8 young per litter; 2 or 3 litters per year. Average life span likely to be only a few months, but in captivity can live at least 2 years

**Related endangered species:** Poncelet's giant rat (*Solomys ponceleti*) EN; Anthony's wood rat (*Neotoma anthonyi*) EN; western small-toothed rat of Indonesia (*Macruromys elegans*) CR; Balkans mole-rat (*Spalax graecus*)* VU; Florida mouse (*Podomys floridanus*) VU

**Status:** Not listed by IUCN; not listed by CITES

**See also:** Categories of Threat 1: 14; Populations 1: 20; Island Biogeography 1: 30; Dormouse, Common 4: 30

apart from some house mice, which died out soon after people left the island in 1930.

## Adapt and Survive

Left to themselves and cut off from the typical wood mice of the mainland with whom they would have bred, the island mice gradually changed to suit their new home. Over many generations they became better adapted to the windswept, rainy conditions on their treeless island. Their fur is now dense and woolly, quite unlike the sleek, thin coat of mainland mice. They also grew much larger than their mainland relatives—more than twice the size. They became quite tame too, having nothing to fear from predators. St. Kilda mice now look quite different from common wood mice, having changed by natural processes.

## Isolated Populations

The IUCN lists more than 125 other rat and mouse species of the family Muridae (that to which the St. Kilda mouse belongs) classified as Endangered or Critically Endangered. Often they, like the St. Kilda mouse, live in small numbers in remote places. Many have evolved to be different precisely because of the remoteness of their populations

on islands, mountaintops, or in other isolated patches of habitat. Isolation tends to cause change, and it happens fastest in the smaller species of mammals, particularly mice, because they breed very quickly. Each generation takes a small step toward the creation of a new form.

Isolated habitats tend to generate new forms of small mammals that are found nowhere else. Often they are not properly studied because their remote homes are rarely visited. Sometimes such peculiar creatures are not seen for decades and are known only from a few skins and skulls in museums, perhaps collected over a half-century ago. The extinction of such species would take away fascinating examples of evolution in action.

**The St. Kilda mouse** *evolved from the common wood mouse. It lives on a windswept island, sheltering among the ruined buildings left behind after people moved away.*

# Mulgara

## *Dasycercus cristicauda*

*Mulgara numbers fluctuate widely throughout much of their range. Nevertheless, there is little doubt that in the 200 years since Europeans settled in Australia, the mulgara's range has shrunk and the population declined.*

The status of the ratlike mulgara of central Australia is something of a mystery. It seems that local mulgara populations are prone to dramatic peaks and troughs, probably brought on by the unpredictable rains and droughts in their desert habitat. The mulgara population is more stable in some parts of its range than in others. It is considered common in the Northern Territories of central Australia, for example, while the few mulgara populations in neighboring Queensland fluctuate wildly; they are sometimes thought to be extinct, only to reappear at a later date.

To add to the confusion, it now seems that many of the animals formerly regarded as mulgaras may, in fact, be a different species, known as the ampurta. Ampurtas live in the east of the mulgara's range, and it is virtually impossible to tell the two types—be they species or subspecies—apart except by analysis of their DNA.

### Shrinking Range

Mulgaras were once common over a wide area, including what are now the Northern Territories, South Australia, and Western Australia. There were also stable populations in Queensland and New South Wales. The only place they appear to be doing well now is the Northern Territories. Isolated populations survive in parts of Western Australia and also in a few sites on the borders of the Northern Territories with Queensland and South Australia.

---

## DATA PANEL

**Mulgara (crest-tailed marsupial mouse)**

*Dasycercus cristicauda*

**Family:** Dasyuridae

**World population:** Unknown; thought to fluctuate widely

**Distribution:** Widespread, but patchy in Western Australia, southern Northern Territories, and northern South Australia

**Habitat:** Sandy, semiarid grasslands

**Size:** Length: 5–8 in (12.5–22 cm); tail: 3–5 in (7–13 cm); males up to twice as large as females. Weight: 2–6 oz (60–170 g)

**Form:** Sandy-brown, ratlike marsupial; crest of black hairs blends into black fur on second half of tail; female lacks true pouch

**Diet:** Small mammals, reptiles, and invertebrates; seeds and root tubers

**Breeding:** Between 6 and 8 young born in May–June after 4-week gestation; remain attached to teat in fold of skin on belly for up to 2 months; independent at 4 months. Life span unknown

**Related endangered species:** Several other small species of insectivorous marsupial in Australia and New Guinea listed as VU or EN

**Status:** IUCN VU; not listed by CITES

---

**See also:** Boom and Bust **1:** 21; Specialization **1:** 28; Dunnart, Kangaroo Island **4:** 50; Numbat **7:** 14

The main causes of decline are predation by dingoes and introduced cats and dogs. The mulgara's habitat has also been altered and destroyed in places. The largest and best-known population is protected in the Uluru-Kata Tjita National Park in the Northern Territories, but even here not enough is known about the precise requirements of the mulgaras to ensure that the land is managed appropriately.

## Picky Eaters

Mulgaras appear to be extremely fussy about their habitat. They live in burrows dug in dry, sandy soils and hunt for food among shoots of spinifex (a spiny-leaved inland grass also known as porcupine grass). However, mulgaras appear to prefer clumps that are about 10 years old, moving on when the centers of large old clumps begin to die off. They also avoid the new growth that springs up in the years after the grasses have been burned. Livestock farmers use regular controlled burning to keep down scrub and to encourage the growth of fresh new grass to feed their cattle and sheep. Cycles of natural burning and regrowth are a normal part of the mulgara's habitat; but when the farmers artificially set fire to the vegetation, the cycles are shorter. As a result, the spinifex rarely has long enough to develop and mature to the mulgaras' satisfaction.

The specific conditions favored by the mulgara are similar to those required by two other vulnerable Australian animals, the southern marsupial mole and the great desert skink (a type of lizard). Currently, conservationists are working on plans for controlling predators and maintaining suitable habitat that will benefit all three species.

*The mulgara is small and ratlike in appearance. It feeds mainly on insects and small animals, and has many small, sharp teeth.*

# Glossary

Words in SMALL CAPITALS refer to other entries in the glossary.

**Adaptation** features of an animal that adjust it to its environment; may be produced by evolution—e.g., camouflage coloration

**Adaptive radiation** where a group of closely related animals (e.g., members of a FAMILY) have evolved differences from each other so that they can survive in different NICHES

**Adhesive disks** flattened disks on the tips of the fingers or toes of certain climbing AMPHIBIANS that enable them to cling to smooth, vertical surfaces

**Adult** a fully grown sexually mature animal; a bird in its final PLUMAGE

**Algae** primitive plants ranging from microscopic, single-celled forms to large forms, such as seaweeds, but lacking proper roots or leaves

**Alpine** living in mountainous areas, usually over 5,000 feet (1,500 m)

**Ambient** describing the conditions around an animal, e.g., the water temperature for a fish or the air temperature for a land animal

**Amphibian** any cold-blooded VERTEBRATE of the CLASS Amphibia, typically living on land but breathing in the water; e.g., frogs, toads, newts, salamanders

**Amphibious** able to live on both land and in water

**Amphipod** a type of CRUSTACEAN found on land and in both fresh and seawater

**Anadromous** fish that spend most of their life at sea but MIGRATE into fresh water for breeding, e.g., salmon

**Annelid** of the PHYLUM Annelida in which the body is made up of similar segments, e.g., earthworms, lugworms, leeches

**Anterior** the front part of an animal

**Arachnid** one of a group of ARTHROPODS of the CLASS Arachnida, characterized by simple eyes and four pairs of legs. Includes spiders and scorpions

**Arboreal** living in trees

**Aristotle's lantern** complex chewing apparatus of sea-urchins that includes five teeth

**Arthropod** the largest PHYLUM in the animal kingdom in terms of the number of SPECIES in it. Characterized by a hard, jointed EXOSKELETON and paired jointed legs. Includes INSECTS, spiders, crabs, etc.

**Baleen** horny substance commonly known as whalebone and growing as plates in the mouth of certain whales; used as a fringelike sieve for extracting plankton from seawater

**Bill** often called the beak: the jaws of a bird, consisting of two bony MANDIBLES, upper and lower, and their horny sheaths

**Biodiversity** the variety of SPECIES and the variation within them

**Biome** a major world landscape characterized by having similar plants and animals living in it, e.g., DESERT, jungle, forest

**Biped** any animal that walks on two legs. *See* QUADRUPED

**Blowhole** the nostril opening on the head of a whale through which it breathes

**Breeding season** the entire cycle of reproductive activity, from courtship, pair formation (and often establishment of territory) through nesting to independence of young

**Bristle** in birds a modified feather, with a bare or partly bare shaft, like a stiff hair; functions include protection, as with eyelashes of ostriches and hornbills, and touch sensors to help catch INSECTS, as with flycatchers

**Brood** the young hatching from a single CLUTCH of eggs

**Browsing** feeding on leaves of trees and shrubs

**Cage bird** A bird kept in captivity; in this set it usually refers to birds taken from the wild

**Canine tooth** a sharp stabbing tooth usually longer than the rest

**Canopy** continuous (closed) or broken (open) layer in forests produced by the intermingling of branches of trees

**Carapace** the upper part of a shell in a CHELONIAN

**Carnivore** meat-eating animal

**Carrion** rotting flesh of dead animals

**Casque** the raised portion on the head of certain REPTILES and birds

**Catadromous** fish that spend most of their life in fresh water but MIGRATE to the sea for SPAWNING, e.g., eels

**Caudal fin** the tail fin in fish

**Cephalothorax** a body region of CRUSTACEANS formed by the union of the head and THORAX. *See* PROSOMA

**Chelicerae** the first pair of appendages ("limbs") on the PROSOMA of spiders, scorpions, etc. Often equipped to inject venom

**Chelonian** any REPTILE of the ORDER Chelonia, including the tortoises and turtles, in which most of the body is enclosed in a bony capsule

**Chrysalis** the PUPA in moths and butterflies

**Class** a large TAXONOMIC group of related animals. MAMMALS, INSECTS, and REPTILES are all CLASSES of animals

**Cloaca** cavity in the pelvic region into which the alimentary canal, genital, and urinary ducts open

**Cloud forest** moist, high-altitude forest characterized by a dense UNDERSTORY and an abundance of ferns, mosses, and other plants growing on the trunks and branches of trees

**Clutch** a set of eggs laid by a female bird in a single breeding attempt

**Cocoon** the protective coat of many insect LARVAE before they develop into PUPAE or the silken covering secreted to protect the eggs

**Colonial** living together in a colony

**Coniferous forest** evergreen forests found in northern regions and mountainous areas, dominated by pines, spruce, and cedars

**Costal** riblike

**Costal grooves** grooves running around the body of some TERRESTRIAL salamanders; they conduct water from the ground to the upper parts of the body

**Coverts** small feathers covering the bases of a bird's main flight feathers on the wings and tail, providing a smooth, streamlined surface for flight

**Crustacean** member of a CLASS within the PHYLUM Arthropoda typified by five pairs of legs, two pairs of antennae, a joined head and THORAX, and calcerous deposits in the EXOSKELETON; e.g., crabs, shrimps, etc.

**Deciduous forest** dominated by trees that lose their leaves in winter (or in the dry season)

**Deforestation** the process of cutting down and removing trees for timber or to create open space for growing crops, grazing animals, etc.

**Desert** area of low rainfall typically with sparse scrub or grassland vegetation or lacking it altogether

**Diatoms** microscopic single-celled ALGAE

**Dispersal** the scattering of young animals going to live away from where they were born and brought up

**Diurnal** active during the day

**DNA** (deoxyribonucleic acid) the substance that makes up the main part of the chromosomes of all living things; contains the genetic code that is handed down from generation to generation

**Domestication** process of taming and breeding animals to provide help and useful products for humans

**Dormancy** a state in which—as a result of hormone action—growth is suspended and METABOLIC activity is reduced to a minimum

**Dorsal** relating to the back or spinal part of the body; usually the upper surface

**Down** soft, fluffy, insulating feathers with few or no shafts found after hatching on young birds and in ADULTS beneath the main feathers

**Echolocation** the process of perception based on reaction to the pattern of reflected sound waves (echos); occurs in bats

**Ecology** the study of plants and animals in relation to one another and to their surroundings

**Ecosystem** a whole system in which plants, animals, and their environment interact

**Ectotherm** animal that relies on external heat sources to raise body temperature; also known as "cold-blooded"

**Edentate** toothless; also any animals of the order Edentata, which includes anteaters, sloths, and armadillos

**Endemic** found only in one geographical area, nowhere else

**Epitoke** a form of marine ANNELID having particularly well developed swimming appendages

**Estivation** inactivity or greatly decreased activity during hot weather

**Eutrophication** an increase in the nutrient chemicals (nitrate, phosphate, etc.) in water, sometimes occurring naturally and sometimes caused by human activities, e.g., by the release of sewage or agricultural fertilizers

**Exoskeleton** a skeleton covering the outside of the body or situated in the skin, as found in some INVERTEBRATES

**Explosive breeding** in some AMPHIBIANS when breeding is completed over one or a very few days and nights

**Extinction** process of dying out at the end of which the very last individual dies, and the SPECIES is lost forever

**Family** a group of closely related SPECIES that often also look quite similar. Zoological FAMILY names always end in -idae. Also used to describe a social group within a SPECIES comprising parents and their offspring

**Feral** domestic animals that have gone wild and live independently of people

**Flagship species** A high-profile SPECIES, which (if present) is likely to be accompanied by many others that are typical of the habitat. (If a naval flagship is present, so is the rest of the fleet of warships and support vessels)

**Fledging period** the period between a young bird hatching and acquiring its first full set of feathers and being able to fly

**Fledgling** young bird that is capable of flight; in perching birds and some others it corresponds with the time of leaving the nest

**Fluke** either of the two lobes of the tail of a whale or related animal; also a type of flatworm, usually parasitic

**Gamebird** birds in the ORDER Galliformes (megapodes, cracids, grouse, partridges, quail, pheasants, and relatives); also used for any birds that may be legally hunted by humans

**Gene** the basic unit of heredity, enabling one generation to pass on characteristics to its offspring

**Genus (genera, pl.)** a group of closely related SPECIES

**Gestation** the period of pregnancy in MAMMALS, between fertilization of the egg and birth of the baby

**Gill** Respiratory organ that absorbs oxygen from the water. External gills occur in tadpoles. Internal gills occur in most fish

**Harem** a group of females living in the same territory and consorting with a single male

**Hen** any female bird

**Herbivore** an animal that eats plants (grazers and BROWSERS are herbivores)

**Hermaphrodite** an animal having both male and female reproductive organs

**Herpetologist** ZOOLOGIST who studies REPTILES and AMPHIBIANS

**Hibernation** becoming inactive in winter, with lowered body temperature to save energy. Hibernation takes place in a special nest or den called a hibernaculum

**Homeotherm** an animal that can maintain a high and constant body temperature by means of internal

processes; also called "warm-blooded"

**Home range** the area that an animal uses in the course of its normal activity

**Hybrid** offspring of two closely related SPECIES that can breed; it is sterile and so cannot produce offspring

**Ichthyologist** ZOOLOGIST specializing in the study of fish

**Inbreeding** breeding among closely related animals (e.g., cousins), leading to weakened genetic composition and reduced survival rates

**Incubation** the act of keeping the egg or eggs warm or the period from the laying of eggs to hatching

**Indwellers** ORGANISMS that live inside others, e.g., the California Bay pea crab, which lives in the tubes of some marine ANNELID worms, but do not act as PARASITES

**Indigenous** living naturally in a region; native (i.e.,not an introduced SPECIES)

**Insect** any air-breathing ARTHROPOD of the CLASS Insecta, having a body divided into head, THORAX, and abdomen, three pairs of legs, and sometimes two pairs of wings

**Insectivore** animal that feeds on INSECTS. Also used as a group name for hedgehogs, shrews, moles, etc.

**Interbreeding** breeding between animals of different SPECIES, varieties, etc. within a single FAMILY or strain; Interbreeding can cause dilution of the GENE pool

**Interspecific** between SPECIES

**Intraspecific** between individuals of the same SPECIES

**Invertebrates** animals that have no backbone (or other bones) inside their body, e.g., mollusks, INSECTS, jellyfish, crabs

**Iridescent** displaying glossy colors produced (e.g., in bird PLUMAGE) not as a result of pigments but by the splitting of sunlight into light of different wavelengths; rainbows are made in the same way

**Joey** a young kangaroo living in its mother's pouch

**Juvenile** a young animal that has not yet reached breeding age

**Keel** a ridge along the CARAPACE of certain turtles or a ridge on the scales of some REPTILES

**Keratin** tough, fibrous material that forms hair, feathers, nails, and

protective plates on the skin of VERTEBRATE animals

**Keystone species** a SPECIES on which many other SPECIES are wholly or partially dependent

**Krill** PLANKTONIC shrimps

**Labyrinth** specialized auxiliary (extra) breathing organ found in some fish

**Larva** an immature form of an animal that develops into an ADULT form through METAMORPHOSIS

**Lateral line system** a system of pores running along a fish's body. These pores lead to nerve endings that allow a fish to sense vibrations in the water and help it locate prey, detect PREDATORS, avoid obstacles, and so on. Also found in AMPHIBIANS

**Lek** communal display area where male birds of some SPECIES gather to attract and mate with females

**Livebearer** animal that gives birth to fully developed young (usually refers to REPTILES or fish)

**Mammal** any animal of the CLASS Mammalia—warm-blooded VERTEBRATE having mammary glands in the female that produce milk with which it nurses its young. The class includes bats, primates, rodents, and whales

**Mandible** upper or lower part of a bird's beak or BILL; also the jawbone in VERTEBRATES; in INSECTS and other ARTHROPODS mandibles are mouth parts mostly used for biting and chewing

**Mantle cavity** a space in the body of mollusks that contains the breathing organs

**Marine** living in the sea

**Matriarch** senior female member of a social group

**Metabolic rate** the rate at which chemical activities occur within animals, including the exchange of gasses in respiration and the liberation of energy from food

**Metamorphosis** the transformation of a LARVA into an ADULT

**Migration** movement from one place to another and back again; usually seasonal

**Molt** the process in which a bird sheds its feathers and replaces them with new ones; some MAMMALS, REPTILES, and ARTHROPODS regularly molt, shedding hair, skin, or outer layers

**Monotreme** egg-laying MAMMAL, e.g., platypus

**Montane** in a mountain environment

**Natural selection** the process

whereby individuals with the most appropriate ADAPTATIONS are more successful than other individuals and therefore survive to produce more offspring. Natural selection is the main process driving evolution in which animals and plants are challenged by natural effects (such as predation and bad weather), resulting in survival of the fittest

**Nematocyst** the stinging part of animals such as jellyfish, usually found on the tentacles

**Nestling** a young bird still in the nest and dependent on its parents

**New World** the Americas

**Niche** part of a habitat occupied by an ORGANISM, defined in terms of all aspects of its lifestyle

**Nocturnal** active at night

**Nomadic** animals that have no fixed home, but wander continuously

**Noseleaf** fleshy structures around the face of bats; helps focus ULTRASOUNDS used for ECHOLOCATION

**Ocelli** markings on an animal's body that resemble eyes. Also, the tiny, simple eyes of some INSECTS, spiders, CRUSTACEANS, mollusks, etc.

**Old World** non-American continents

**Olfaction** sense of smell

**Operculum** a cover consisting of bony plates that covers the GILLS of fish

**Omnivore** an animal that eats a wide range of both animal and vegetable food

**Order** a subdivision of a CLASS of animals, consisting of a series of animal FAMILIES

**Organism** any member of the animal or plant kingdom; a body that has life

**Ornithologist** ZOOLOGIST specializing in the study of birds

**Osteoderms** bony plates beneath the scales of some REPTILES, particularly crocodilians

**Oviparous** producing eggs that hatch outside the body of the mother (in fish, REPTILES, birds, and MONOTREMES)

**Parasite** an animal or plant that lives on or within the body of another (the host) from which it obtains nourishment. The host is often harmed by the association

**Passerine** any bird of the ORDER Passeriformes; includes SONGBIRDS

**Pedipalps** small, paired leglike appendages immediately in front of the first pair of walking legs of spiders and other ARACHNIDS. Used by males for transferring sperm to the females

**Pelagic** living in the upper waters of the open sea or large lakes

**Pheromone** scent produced by animals to enable others to find and recognize them

**Photosynthesis** the production of food in green plants using sunlight as an energy source and water plus carbon dioxide as raw materials

**Phylum** zoological term for a major grouping of animal CLASSES. The whole animal kingdom is divided into about 30 PHYLA, of which the VERTEBRATES form part of just one

**Placenta** the structure that links an embryo to its mother during pregnancy, allowing exchange of chemicals between them

**Plankton** animals and plants drifting in open water; many are minute

**Plastron** the lower shell of CHELONIANS

**Plumage** the covering of feathers on a bird's body

**Plume** a long feather used for display, as in a bird of paradise

**Polygamous** where an individual has more than one mate in one BREEDING SEASON. Monogamous animals have only a single mate

**Polygynous** where a male mates with several females in one BREEDING SEASON

**Polyp** individual ORGANISM that lives as part of a COLONY—e.g., a coral—with a saclike body opening only by the mouth that is usually surrounded by a ring of tentacles

**Population** a distinct group of animals of the same SPECIES or all the animals of that SPECIES

**Posterior** the hind end or behind another structure

**Predator** an animal that kills live prey

**Prehensile** capable of grasping

**Primary forest** forest that has always been forest and has not been cut down and regrown at some time

**Primates** a group of MAMMALS that includes monkeys, apes, and ourselves

**Prosoma** the joined head and THORAX of a spider, scorpion, or horseshoe crab

**Pupa** an INSECT in the stage of METAMORPHOSIS between a caterpillar (LARVA) and an ADULT (imago)

**Quadruped** any animal that walks on four legs

**Range** the total geographical area over which a SPECIES is distributed

**Raptor** bird with hooked beak and strong feet with sharp claws (talons) for seizing, killing, and dealing with prey; also known as birds of prey. The term usually refers to daytime birds of prey (eagles, hawks, falcons, and relatives) but sometimes also includes NOCTURNAL owls

**Regurgitate** (of a bird) to vomit partly digested food either to feed NESTLINGS or to rid itself of bones, fur, or other indigestible parts, or (in some seabirds) to scare off PREDATORS

**Reptile** any member of the cold-blooded CLASS Reptilia, such as crocodiles, lizards, snakes, tortoises, turtles, and tuataras; characterized by an external covering of scales or horny plates. Most are egg-layers, but some give birth to fully developed young

**Roost** place that a bird or bat regularly uses for sleeping

**Ruminant** animals that eat vegetation and later bring it back from the stomach to chew again ("chewing the cud") to assist its digestion by microbes in the stomach

**Savanna** open grasslands with scattered trees and low rainfall, usually in warm areas

**Scapulars** the feathers of a bird above its shoulders

**Scent** chemicals produced by animals to leave smell messages for others to find and interpret

**Scrub** vegetation dominated by shrubs—woody plants usually with more than one stem

**Scute** horny plate covering live body tissue underneath

**Secondary forest** trees that have been planted or grown up on cleared ground

**Sedge** grasslike plant

**Shorebird** Plovers, sandpipers, and relatives (known as waders in Britain, Australia, and some other areas)

**Slash-and-burn agriculture** method of farming in which the unwanted vegetation is cleared by cutting down and burning

**Social behavior** interactions between individuals within the same SPECIES, e.g., courtship

**Songbird** member of major bird group of PASSERINES

**Spawning** the laying and fertilizing of eggs by fish and AMPHIBIANS and some mollusks

**Speciation** the origin of SPECIES; the diverging of two similar ORGANISMS

through reproduction down through the generations into different forms resulting in a new SPECIES

**Species** a group of animals that look similar and can breed with each other to produce fertile offspring

**Steppe** open grassland in parts of the world where the climate is too harsh for trees to grow

**Subspecies** a subpopulation of a single SPECIES whose members are similar to each other but differ from the typical form for that SPECIES; often called a race

**Substrate** a medium to which fixed animals are attached under water, such as rocks onto which barnacles and mussels are attached, or plants are anchored in, e.g., gravel, mud, or sand in which AQUATIC plants have their roots embedded

**Substratum** see SUBSTRATE

**Swim bladder** a gas or air-filled bladder in fish; by taking in or exhaling air, the fish can alter its buoyancy

**Symbiosis** a close relationship between members of two SPECIES from which both partners benefit

**Taxonomy** the branch of biology concerned with classifying ORGANISMS into groups according to similarities in their structure, origins, or behavior. The categories, in order of increasing broadness, are: SPECIES, GENUS, FAMILY, ORDER, CLASS, PHYLUM

**Terrestrial** living on land

**Territory** defended space

**Test** an external covering or "shell" of an INVERTEBRATE such as a sea-urchin; it is in fact an internal skeleton just below the skin

**Thorax** (**thoracic**, adj.) in an INSECT the middle region of the body between the head and the abdomen. It bears the wings and three pairs of walking legs

**Torpor** deep sleep accompanied by lowered body temperature and reduced METABOLIC RATE

**Translocation** transferring members of a SPECIES from one location to another

**Tundra** open grassy or shrub-covered lands of the far north

**Underfur** fine hairs forming a dense, woolly mass close to the skin and underneath the outer coat of stiff hairs in MAMMALS

**Understory** the layer of shrubs,

herbs, and small trees found beneath the forest CANOPY

**Ungulate** one of a large group of hoofed animals such as pigs, deer, cattle, and horses; mostly HERBIVORES

**Uterus** womb in which embryos of MAMMALS develop

**Ultrasounds** sounds that are too high-pitched for humans to hear

**UV-B radiation** component of ultraviolet radiation from the sun that is harmful to living ORGANISMS because it breaks up DNA

**Vane** the bladelike main part of a typical bird feather extending from either side of its shaft (midrib)

**Ventral** of or relating to the front part or belly of an animal (see DORSAL)

**Vertebrate** animal with a backbone (e.g., fish, MAMMAL, REPTILE), usually with skeleton made of bones, but sometimes softer cartilage

**Vestigial** a characteristic with little or no use, but derived from one that was well developed in an ancestral form; e.g., the "parson's nose" (the fatty end portion of the tail when a fowl is cooked) is the compressed bones from the long tail of the reptilian ancestor of birds

**Viviparous** (of most MAMMALS and a few other VERTEBRATES) giving birth to active young rather than laying eggs

**Waterfowl** members of the bird FAMILY Anatidae, the swans, geese, and ducks; sometimes used to include other groups of wild AQUATIC birds

**Wattle** fleshy protuberance, usually near the base of a bird's BILL

**Wingbar** line of contrasting feathers on a bird's wing

**Wing case** one of the protective structures formed from the first pair of nonfunctional wings, which are used to protect the second pair of functional wings in INSECTS such as beetles

**Wintering ground** the area where a migrant spends time outside the BREEDING SEASON

**Yolk** part of the egg that contains nourishment for a growing embryo

**Zooid** individual animal in a colony; usually applied to corals or bryozoa (sea-mats)

**Zoologist** person who studies animals

**Zoology** the study of animals

# Further Reading

**Mammals**
Macdonald, David, *The Encyclopedia of Mammals*, Barnes & Noble, New York, U.S., 2001

Payne, Roger, *Among Whales*, Bantam Press, U.S., 1996

Reeves, R. R., and Leatherwood, S., *The Sierra Club Handbook of Whales and Dolphins of the World*, Sierra Club, U.S., 1983

Sherrow, Victoria, and Cohen, Sandee, *Endangered Mammals of North America*, Twenty-First Century Books, U.S., 1995

Whitaker, J. O., *Audubon Society Field Guide to North American Mammals*, Alfred A. Knopf, New York, U.S., 1996

**Birds**
Attenborough, David, *The Life of Birds*, BBC Books, London, U.K., 1998

BirdLife International, *Threatened Birds of the World*, Lynx Edicions, Barcelona, Spain and BirdLife International, Cambridge, U.K., 2000

del Hoyo, J., Elliott, A., and Sargatal, J., eds., *Handbook of Birds of the World* Vols 1 to 6, Lynx Edicions, Barcelona, Spain, 1992–2001

Sayre, April Pulley, *Endangered Birds of North America*, Scientific American Sourcebooks, Twenty-First Century Books, U.S., 1977

Scott, Shirley L., ed., *A Field Guide to the Birds of North America*, National Geographic, U.S., 1999

Stattersfield, A., Crosby, M., Long, A., and Wege, D., eds., *Endemic Bird Areas of the World: Priorities for Biodiversity Conservation*, BirdLife International, Cambridge, U.K., 1998

Thomas, Peggy, *Bird Alert: Science of Saving*, Twenty-First Century Books, U.S., 2000

**Fish**
Bannister, Keith, and Campbell, Andrew, *The Encyclopedia of Aquatic Life*, Facts On File, New York, U.S., 1997

Buttfield, Helen, *The Secret Lives of Fishes*, Abrams, U.S., 2000

**Reptiles and Amphibians**
Corbett, Keith, *Conservation of European Reptiles and Amphibians*, Christopher Helm, London, U.K., 1989

Corton, Misty, *Leopard and Other South African Tortoises*, Carapace Press, London, U.K., 2000

Hofrichter, Robert, *Amphibians: The World of Frogs, Toads, Salamanders, and Newts*, Firefly Books, Canada, 2000

Stafford, Peter, *Snakes*, Natural History Museum, London, U.K., 2000

**Insects**
Borror, Donald J., and White, Richard E., *A Field Guide to Insects: America, North of Mexico*, Houghton Mifflin, New York, U.S., 1970

Pyle, Robert Michael, *National Audubon Society Field Guide to North American Butterflies*, Alfred A. Knopf, New York, U.S., 1995

**General**
Adams, Douglas, and Carwardine, Mark, *Last Chance to See*, Random House, London, U.K., 1992

Allaby, Michael, *The Concise Oxford Dictionary of Ecology*, Oxford University Press, Oxford, U.K., 1998

Douglas, Dougal, and others, *Atlas of Life on Earth*, Barnes & Noble, New York, U.S., 2001

National Wildlife Federation, *Endangered Species: Wild and Rare*, McGraw-Hill, U.S., 1996

# Websites

http://www.abcbirds.org/ American Bird Conservancy. Articles, information about campaigns and bird conservation in the Americas

http://elib.cs.berkeley.edu/aw/ AmphibiaWeb information about amphibians and their conservation

http://animaldiversity.ummz.umich.edu/ University of Michigan Museum of Zoology animal diversity web. Search for pictures and information about animals by class, family, and common name. Includes glossary

www.beachside.org sea turtle preservation society

http://www.birdlife.net BirdLife International, an alliance of conservation organizations working in more than 100 countries to save birds and their habitats

http://www.surfbirds.com Articles, mystery photographs, news, book reviews, birding polls, and more

http://www.birds.cornell.edu/ Cornell University. Courses, news, nest-box cam

http://www.cites.org/ CITES and IUCN listings. Search for animals by scientific name of order, family, genus, species, or common name. Location by country and explanation of reasons for listings

www.ufl.edu/natsci/herpetology/crocs.htm crocodile site, including a chat room

www.darwinfoundation.org/ Charles Darwin Research Center

http://www.open.cc.uk/daptf DAPTF–Decllining Amphibian Population Task Force. Providing information and data about amphibian declines. (International Director, Professor Tim Halliday, is co-author of this set)

http://www.ucmp.berkeley.edu/echinodermata the echinoderm phylum—starfish, sea-urchins, etc.

http://endangered.fws.gov information about endangered animals and plants from the U.S. Fish and Wildlife Service, the organization in charge of 94 million acres of wildlife refuges

http://forests.org/ includes forest conservation answers to queries

www.traffic.org/turtles freshwater turtles

www.iucn.org details of species, IUCN listings and IUCN publications

http://www.pbs.org/journeytoamazonia the Amazonian rain forest and its unrivaled biodiversity

http://www.audubon.org National Audubon Society, named after the ornithologist and wildlife artist John James Audubon (1785–1851). Sections on education, local Audubon societies, and bird identification

www.nccnsw.org.au site for threatened Australian species

http://cmc-ocean.org facts, figures, and quizzes about marine life

http://wwwl.nature.nps.gov/wv/ The U.S. National Park Service wildlife and plants site. Factsheets on all kinds of animals found in the parks

www.ewt.org.za endangered South African wildlife

http://www.panda.org World Wide Fund for Nature (WWF). Newsroom, press releases, government reports, campaigns. Themed photogallery

http://www.greenchannel.com/wwt/ Wildfowl and Wetlands Trust (U.K.). Founded by artist and naturalist Sir Peter Scott, the trust aims to preserve wetlands for rare waterbirds. Includes information on places to visit and threatened waterbird species

http://wdcs.org/ Whale and Dolphin Conservation Society site. News, projects, and campaigns. Sightings database

# List of Animals by Group

Listed below are the common names of the animals featured in the A–Z part of this set grouped by their class, i.e., Mammals, Birds, Fish, Reptiles, Amphibians, and Insects and Invertebrates.

**Bold** numbers indicate the volume number and are followed by the first page number of the two-page illustrated main entry in the set.

## Mammals
addax **2**:4
anoa, mountain **2**:20
anteater, giant **2**:24
antelope, Tibetan **2**:26
armadillo, giant **2**:30
ass
  African wild **2**:34
  Asiatic wild **2**:36
aye-aye **2**:42
babirusa **2**:44
baboon, gelada **2**:46
bandicoot, western barred **2**:48
banteng **2**:50
bat
  ghost **2**:56
  gray **2**:58
  greater horseshoe **2**:60
  greater mouse-eared **2**:62
  Kitti's hog-nosed **2**:64
  Morris's **2**:66
bear
  grizzly **2**:68
  polar **2**:70
  sloth **2**:72
  spectacled **2**:74
beaver, Eurasian **2**:76
bison
  American **2**:86
  European **2**:88
blackbuck **2**:94
camel, wild bactrian **3**:24
cat, Iriomote **3**:30
cheetah **3**:40
chimpanzee **3**:42
  pygmy **3**:44
chinchilla, short-tailed **3**:46
cow, Steller's sea **3**:70
cuscus, black-spotted **3**:86
deer
  Chinese water **4**:6
  Kuhl's **4**:8
  Père David's **4**:10
  Siberian musk **4**:12
desman, Russian **4**:14
dhole **4**:16
dog
  African wild **4**:22

bush **4**:24
dolphin
  Amazon river **4**:26
  Yangtze river **4**:28
dormouse
  common **4**:30
  garden **4**:32
  Japanese **4**:34
drill **4**:40
dugong **4**:46
duiker, Jentink's **4**:48
dunnart, Kangaroo Island **4**:50
echidna, long-beaked **4**:60
elephant
  African **4**:64
  Asian **4**:66
elephant-shrew, golden-rumped **4**:68
ferret, black-footed **4**:72
flying fox
  Rodrigues (Rodriguez) **4**:84
  Ryukyu **4**:86
fossa **4**:90
fox, swift **4**:92
gaur **5**:18
gazelle, dama **5**:20
gibbon, black **5**:26
giraffe, reticulated **5**:30
glider, mahogany **5**:32
gorilla
  mountain **5**:38
  western lowland **5**:40
gymnure, Hainan **5**:48
hare, hispid **5**:50
hippopotamus, pygmy **5**:52
horse, Przewalski's wild **5**:58
hutia, Jamaican **5**:64
hyena
  brown **5**:66
  spotted **5**:68
ibex, Nubian **5**:70
indri **5**:84
jaguar **5**:86
koala **6**:10
kouprey **6**:14
kudu, greater **6**:16
lemur
  hairy-eared dwarf **6**:22
  Philippine flying **6**:24
  ruffed **6**:26
leopard **6**:28
  clouded **6**:30
  snow **6**:32
lion, Asiatic **6**:34
loris, slender **6**:46
lynx, Iberian **6**:52
macaque
  barbary **6**:54
  Japanese **6**:56
manatee, Florida **6**:68
markhor **6**:72
marten, pine **6**:74
mink, European **6**:78

mole, marsupial **6**:80
mole-rat
  Balkans **6**:82
  giant **6**:84
monkey
  douc **6**:86
  Goeldi's **6**:88
  proboscis **6**:90
mouse, St. Kilda **6**:92
mulgara **6**:94
numbat **7**:14
nyala, mountain **7**:18
ocelot, Texas **7**:20
okapi **7**:22
orang-utan **7**:26
oryx
  Arabian **7**:28
  scimitar-horned **7**:30
otter
  European **7**:32
  giant **7**:34
  sea **7**:36
ox, Vu Quang **7**:44
panda
  giant **7**:48
  lesser **7**:50
pangolin, long-tailed **7**:52
panther, Florida **7**:54
pig, Visayan warty **7**:68
pika, steppe **7**:74
platypus **7**:82
porpoise, harbor **7**:86
possum, Leadbeater's **7**:88
potoroo, long-footed **7**:90
prairie dog, black-tailed **7**:92
pygmy-possum, mountain **8**:4
quagga **8**:8
rabbit
  Amami **8**:12
  volcano **8**:14
rat, black **8**:24
rhinoceros
  black **8**:26
  great Indian **8**:28
  Javan **8**:30
  Sumatran **8**:32
  white **8**:34
rock-wallaby, Prosperine **8**:36
saiga **8**:42
sea lion, Steller's **8**:62
seal
  Baikal **8**:70
  gray **8**:72
  Hawaiian monk **8**:74
  Mediterranean monk **8**:76
  northern fur **8**:78
sheep, barbary **8**:88
shrew, giant otter **8**:90
sifaka, golden-crowned **8**:92
sloth, maned **9**:6
solenodon, Cuban **9**:16
souslik, European **9**:18
squirrel, Eurasian red **9**:28

tahr, Nilgiri **9**:46
takin **9**:50
tamarin, golden lion **9**:52
tapir
  Central American **9**:56
  Malayan **9**:58
tenrec, aquatic **9**:64
thylacine **9**:66
tiger **9**:68
tree-kangaroo, Goodfellow's **10**:4
vicuña **10**:28
whale
  blue **10**:40
  fin **10**:42
  gray **10**:44
  humpback **10**:46
  killer **10**:48
  minke **10**:50
  northern right **10**:52
  sei **10**:54
  sperm **10**:56
  white **10**:58
wildcat **10**:62
wolf
  Ethiopian **10**:64
  Falkland Island **10**:66
  gray **10**:68
  maned **10**:70
  red **10**:72
wolverine **10**:74
wombat, northern hairy-nosed **10**:76
yak, wild **10**:90
zebra
  Grevy's **10**:92
  mountain **10**:94

## Birds
akiapolaau **2**:6
albatross, wandering **2**:8
amazon, St. Vincent **2**:14
asity, yellow-bellied **2**:32
auk, great **2**:38
barbet, toucan **2**:54
bellbird, three-wattled **2**:82
bird of paradise, blue **2**:84
bittern, Eurasian **2**:90
blackbird, saffron-cowled **2**:92
bowerbird, Archbold's **3**:8
bustard, great **3**:10
cassowary, southern **3**:28
cockatoo, salmon-crested **3**:52
condor, California **3**:60
coot, horned **3**:62
cormorant, Galápagos **3**:64
corncrake **3**:66
courser, Jerdon's **3**:68
crane, whooping **3**:76
crow, Hawaiian **3**:82
curlew, Eskimo **3**:84
dipper, rufous-throated **4**:18

# Set Index

# Acknowledgments

The authors and publishers would like to thank the following people and organizations:
Aquamarines International Pvt. Ltd., Sri Lanka, especially Ananda Pathirana; Aquarist & Pond keeper Magazine, U.K.; BirdLife International (the global partnership of conservation organizations working together in over 100 countries to save birds and their habitats). Special thanks to David Capper; also to Guy Dutson and Alison Stattersfield; Sylvia Clarke (Threatened Wildlife, South Australia); Mark Cocker (writer and birder); David Curran (aquarist specializing in spiny eels, U.K.); Marydele Donnelly (IUCN sea turtle specialist); Svein Fossa (aquatic consultant, Norway); Richard Gibson (Jersey Wildlife Preservation Trust, Channel Islands); Paul Hoskisson (Liverpool John Moores University); Derek Lambert; Pat Lambert (aquarists specializing in freshwater livebearers); Lumbini Aquaria Wayamba Ltd., Sri Lanka, especially Jayantha Ramasinghe and Vibhu Perera; Isolda McGeorge (Chester Zoological Gardens); Dr. James Peron Ross (IUCN crocodile specialist); Zoological Society of London, especially Michael Palmer, Ann Sylph, and the other library staff.

# Picture Credits

## Abbreviations

AL      Ardea London
BBC     BBC Natural History Unit
BCC     Bruce Coleman Collection
FLPA    Frank Lane Photographic Agency
NHPA    Natural History Photographic Agency
OSF     Oxford Scientific Films
PEP     Planet Earth Pictures
**b** = bottom; **c** = center; **t** = top; **l** = left; **r** = right

## Jacket

Ibiza wall lizard, illustration by Denys Ovenden from *Collins Field Guide: Reptiles and Amphibians of Britain and Europe*; Grevy's zebra, Stan Osolinski/Oxford Scientific Films; Florida panther, Lynn M. Stone/BBC Natural History Unit; silver shark, Max Gibbs/Photomax; blue whale, Tui de Roy/Oxford Scientific Films

**4–5** Nick Garbutt/PEP; **6–7** Jorge Sierra/OSF; **9** Mark Jones/OSF; **10–11** Dave Watts; **12–13** Paul Kay/OSF; **16–17** Daryl Balfour/NHPA; **18–19** Rene Pop/Windrush Photos; **21** Martin Dohrn/Science Photo Library; **27** Alan & Sandy Carey/OSF; **27** inset David Haring/OSF; **28–29** Alan & Sandy Carey/OSF; **30–31** Martin Harvey/NHPA; **32–33** Alan & Sandy Carey/OSF; **34–35** Vivek R. Sinha/OSF; **36–37** Animals Animals/John Gerlach/OSF; **40–41** illustration by Denys Ovenden from *Collins Field Guide: Reptiles and Amphibians of Britain and Europe*; **42–43** Daniel Heuclin/NHPA; **44–45** R.A. Preston-Mafham/ Premaphotos Wildlife; **46–47** Stanley Breeden/OSF; **49** Tony Tilford/OSF; **51** A.N.T./NHPA; **53** Rico & Ruiz/BBC; **55** Doug Allan/OSF; **57** Daniel J. Cox/OSF; **59** Stan Osolinski/OSF; **61** Claus Meyer/PEP; **63** Pete Oxford/BBC; **64–65** Survival Anglia/Jen & Des Bartlett/OSF; **68–69** Gerard Soury/OSF; **71** Tom Brakefield/PEP; **73** Anup Shah/BBC; **74–75** Manfred Danegger/NHPA; **77** A. Hawkins/BirdLife International; **78–79** Vadim Sidorovich/BBC; **81** A.N.T./NHPA; **83** Eyal Bartov/OSF; **85** P. Morris; **86–87** Anup Shah; **89** Jurgen & Christine Sohns/FLPA; **91** Animals Animals/Michael Dick/OSF; **93** P. Morris; **94–95** Kathie Atkinson/OSF.

## Artists

Graham Allen, Norman Arlott, Priscilla Barrett, Trevor Boyer, Ad Cameron, David Dennis, Karen Hiscock, Chloe Talbot Kelly, Mick Loates, Michael Long, Malcolm McGregor, Denys Ovenden, Oxford Illustrators, John Sibbick, Joseph Tomelleri, Dick Twinney, Ian Willis

*While every effort has been made to trace the copyright holders of illustrations reproduced in this book, the publishers will be pleased to rectify any omissions or inaccuracies.*